The Child who Fell
from the Sky

Stephan Chadwick

Leaping Boy Publications

Published by Leaping Boy Publications
0044 (0) 1525 222 600
partners@neallscott.co.uk
www.leapingboy.com

Cover design by Rebecca Chapman

Printed and distributed by Lightning Source UK Ltd.

A CIP catalogue record for this title is available
from the British Library.

ISBN 978-0-9926464-9-3

Why I have written this book

I have written this book with the intention of rescuing the child I abandoned many years ago when I was six years old. It is now time for me to share my story in a positive attempt to heal a lifetime searching for understanding, acceptance and love.

This book is an attempt to find a way to understand my feelings of not belonging, and the difficulties and dangers of not being able to read and write as a teenager.

I share my story with you that you may obtain the courage to change, and never give up your magical and wonderfully precious life and ability to be positive and creative.

I seek to make amends with myself and with God. If I am to complete my life with a positive non-violent end, I need to create an act of true love and understanding, with compassion for myself and the human race.

I write this book in an attempt to defuse my deep resentment, defiance and disapproval of humanity and God. I am deeply wounded by the pain and suffering of humanity.

The pen really is mightier than the sword, this I have now come to understand.

Stephan Chadwick

Dedications

I dedicate this book to all the children that know the true meaning of abandonment.

I dedicate this book to all the people that I have hurt, failed and abandoned, too many to name.

I dedicate this book to the very special ones that have tried to love me and suffered for doing so.

I dedicate this book to those that search for truth, light and purpose.

If not for the foolishness of those that govern
with unseeing hearts and minds,
lost in egos and desires of power,
maybe all children would grow to be similarly
unafraid and dynamic
bringing magic into the world,
I heard the Shining One say.

INTRODUCTION

After the War - London, England 1947

Once upon a time, a small child came to the world from the sky. In the years before he arrived there had been a great war raging upon the earth, there had been much cruelty and suffering on the planet and many had died just as they had done many times before. The humans had still not known how to live together in peace. Their greed for control and power over others had been repeated many times in their history and still they had failed to learn from their mistakes and the suffering of the generations that had gone before. There was a powerful tribe known as the Germans. This tribe had been blamed for starting the war, a terrible evil war, just as all wars prove to be. The leaders of the German nation were known to be very cruel and evil. They wanted to take over and rule the world with a superior elite race of humans. They were very clever and built machines that could fly into the sky, carrying their brave warriors and armed with bombs of steel explosives. They would fly over the lands of their victims, dropping their bombs onto the people below.

One of their missions was to drop their bombs on the capital city of England, London, killing as many people as possible, causing fear and panic among the city dwellers. This race of people was called the 'British' and they were also clever and inventive. The British soldiers on the ground would shoot their explosive shells up into the sky towards the flying machines with their big ground guns. The shells they fired would explode in mid-air, shooting metal fragments from their centre, outwards, in all directions.

Sometimes the exploding metal fragments would strike into the flying machines, causing damage and killing the Germans inside, making the machines unable to fly and forcing them to crash down to earth at great speed, exploding on impact. Sometimes the Germans inside, if quick, were able to jump out clear into the open sky enabling them to operate a parachute. This was strapped on their backs and would open up and fill with air, dropping them slowly down towards the ground, saving their lives. This was to become a regular activity for both sides for several years: the fear and hatred grew; the death and suffering of the British people increased; and many flying machines were shot down and destroyed. The Germans in the flying machines were mostly killed, but some survived. The ones lucky enough to survive were quickly captured by the British soldiers waiting on the ground. The captured German aircrew would be taken off to secure interrogation compounds, known as prisoner of war camps.

Two German aircrew were captured and imprisoned until the war ended, at which time they were set free by the British government. They were given a choice: stay in Britain or return to their German homeland across the sea that was now occupied by British, Americans and the Russians, whose policy towards the Germans was particularly brutal. The two German aircrew walked freely among the British people. Everyone was happy and rejoicing that the war was over. Men and women embraced each other with joy, and many would create children together, giving a much-needed boost to the now depleted population. So many people had died and life for the people had become extremely difficult. There was a shortage of food and money. Many houses and homes had been destroyed by the bombs and fire.

The two Germans were careful not to get found out, for they feared the crowds would turn on them and maybe even kill them, so they passed themselves off as Polish aircrew. It was widely known that many Polish had volunteered to fly aircrafts for the British against the Germans in the war, so this would prove to be a safe cover, unless of course they were to meet up with some real Poles. But it was a risk they needed to take if they were to mix with the crowds of young women, which was the main attraction for both of them, and it was not long before they had met two young good looking English girls; two very bold, sexy and unafraid English girls.

The two Germans, passing as Polish, considered themselves to be extremely lucky finding such women, willing to go out with them. To the two young women the young handsome Polish pilots were exciting and romantic. The names of the posing Germans were Peter and Alfred. Alfred, calling himself Fred, was to stay and marry one of the women, having four children together over several years. Peter was to return home to war-torn Germany, now devastated and ruined, leaving behind the other English woman pregnant by him. The child was born and it was to be a boy with blonde curly hair and his name was Stephan. The child's mother was just seventeen years old and lived at home, sharing a room with her fourteen-year-old brother Jack. Their father had recently died and now things were hard; money was short. Kathleen's mother had strict Victorian values. She took the child in, caring for him, and Kathleen was made to leave the house in shame. The child was to take the family name of the grandmother and life went on as normal, no-one knowing any different.

Chapter 1

My first memory of life was blissful, my tiny body fully alive, feeling the warmth of the sun on my face, piercing through my closed eyes. I could see into the glowing yellow redness of the sun. I drifted into a feeling of being somewhere else, a memory of a time before I was born.

Where was this other place? Who was this other person? It was me, and I could hear myself pleading, "Please don't send me back there again. You know how much I hate it there. The sorrow and the sadness, so overwhelming; the hurt and pain is too much to bear. Please don't send me back!"

You must go back one more time. This will be your last time there.

I remember how beautiful and full of joy and love that place was, knowing and seeing all things in a moment of perfect oneness. The oneness of all things from the very beginning to the very end, consisting of everything that ever was and everything that would ever be; light and darkness being the same – difficult to understand.

Still sucking gently on the bottle of warm milk, which melted into my new body, I knew then how important milk was, the food of life, warm milk. I felt safe, protected and very alive, but separate from my small body. I seemed to rise up into the sunlight, out of my pram, up into the air. It felt much like the place I had come from.

How could I know of such a place, beyond imagination and understanding? Had I really come from such a place and was here, a tiny child in a pram? I was alive and I had a life to live. I am OK; it's not so bad. I am safe and when it's done I will return to that wonderful place of love; I have to trust that it won't be too difficult, too painful for me to bear, I will try to enjoy this life. I would never forget I had a place to go back to when I was finished here. I had my return ticket no matter what happened in this lifetime. I was safe.

I continued sucking the milk of life through the rubber teat with grateful expectancy. If only I could hold onto this moment until the end, if only I could – if only.

My eyes close, looking into the sunlight, I hear two women talking. One is my guardian, my grandmother, and the other a neighbour from two doors away from where we live. We are in the public alleyway leading to the shops in the high street.

I am high up above my pram, my eyes still closed. I can see all around, in every direction, clear and very vivid; I can see the local school, so very near, and the chain link fence running between the school playing field and the public walkway. The green grass and the white goalposts at each end of the field. The street where I live with my grandmother over there, and the other houses all around. I can almost see the park behind the houses towards the end of the road, I can see the treetops rising up above the houses into the blue sky. I have seen those trees many times before, looking up from my pram into their branches and out beyond. I look down and see my grandmother speaking to the neighbour. I see myself in the pram and it all feels so normal and safe. We are halfway along the alleyway where there is a dip down and then it rises up again and runs on to the high street, the main road and the bus station. I see all this with vivid detail – a magic moment of bliss – and then I am back in my child's body again and life goes on.

That was to be a special summer, one that I would remember so well – how beautiful and wonderful it was for me. Amazing magical days as I looked up to the sky from the safety of my pram, up through the green leaves and branches which stretched into the wide blue never-ending sky with big white clouds and the sunlight flickering down through the trees, warm on my face.

Here I am safe and cared for in the shadows of the trees, wonderful giant trees, each one different from the one before, then passing into smaller trees, all with colour on them. How I longed to understand; I stared open-eyed, looking and looking that I may see all there was to see and never forget the wonder and beauty of it.

The paddling pool was at the far top corner of the park, southwest from the house – I always seemed to know where I was in relation to the house. A lot of noise came from the pool and faded as we passed. It would be some years yet before I would learn the true nature of the noise that came from the children's pool. For now it was back home to where I live with my grandmother, just me and her it seemed, but there was a strangeness about it all that I did not yet understand; I would learn as the months and years passed by.

I lived with my grandmother for the next three years. She was everything to me – my mother, my guardian and protector. Life was wonderful, just the two of us. I had her all to myself. The bed was soft and warm with crisp clean sheets. The house carried warmth and kindness about it. Food was always readily available twice a day and there was the occasional cuddle. I felt loved and safe.

The house was clean and tidy, with little clutter. The warmth of the fire and the humming of the gaslight in the evening signalled that all was well, it would soon be time to sleep, and a new day was awaiting me. Each day would bring something new for me to see and learn. Life was full of the joy of learning; I was excited by all the possibilities.

There was a garden to explore with many colourful flowers, vegetables and chickens; and regular walks to the park in my pram with my grandmother. All this gave a sense of normality and ease to our daily living.

The chickens were at the very bottom of the garden and as the days and weeks passed I was allowed into the wired compound with them. I would sometimes try to catch hold of them. I was encouraged to search for eggs, and when I found an egg I would pass it quickly on to my grandmother. Later she would boil it in a pan of hot water and then I would eat it, spoonful by spoonful, and between spoonfuls I would dip in my thin strips of bread coated with butter. These were called soldiers. I would dip the soldiers into the warm yellow egg yolk, which sometimes overflowed at the sides, and would quickly try to catch the overflowing yolk with my bread. It tasted wonderful and sometimes I could manage two eggs. At the end of each day I would look forward to the comfort and gentleness of bedtime.

I was well guarded and protected, but at times I felt something was missing; there was a cold sense of secrecy around the house, which I did not understand. Understanding was to come later, my only concern for the moment was my big soft bed with its clean white sheets and the constant attention of this woman called Nan.

Once a week I would get a bath or bed wash, which made me shiver with coldness for a few moments. I remember bath time making my willy go stiff; it felt good just lying there naked on the bed, legs wide open with my maleness sticking up. My nan would rub me down with a big warm white towel, which added to the sensation, and then she would rub white powder all over my body making me feel dry and soft. The dimness of the gaslight, flickering on the wall, and its humming sound made it all feel so safe and blissful. I loved every moment of it and never wanted it to end. Just me and this wonderful, capable, caring woman. It made me feel special. Nothing in the world was going to hurt me; just as long as she was around, I was safe.

The fire would be lit in the early morning, making the house warm. The chickens would have to be fed, another job for me. Maybe I would find some eggs again. What would I get to eat for breakfast I wondered, eggs again probably! The days came and went and the mysteries of the night were unknown to me. My nan would come to share my bed late in the night and leave again early in the morning. She rarely woke me from sleep.

Despite my grandmother's loving care, there was a strange detachment about her, a part that I could not reach. She seemed unavailable and I found myself yearning for something more, and that something, unknown to me, was the bond a child has with its mother. I neither knew nor felt anything of this bond. I had someone that loved and cared for me, but I had no idea who my mother was. This woman was my grandmother who unknown to me had given birth to five children, two of which were twins, one of them dying at birth. So who was this person that cared for me so wonderfully? Many times I tried to see behind the glass windows on her face and failed to do so. Each time I searched to see into her eyes, I could not find her. She was not there. I could not touch her. There was an emptiness about her. She was strangely quiet. I learnt very little about her, other than what I could see. She wore thin cotton frocks with flower patterns on them, with an over-apron to the front of her body that was tied at the back. She would use this when cooking and cleaning, and washing up. She listened to the radio, which would be more often on than off, voices talking, songs and music quietly coming from a brown wooden box with three buttons on the front that I was not allowed to touch.

I would spend more and more time in the garden with my new tricycle, peddling my way around, down to the chicken house, in search of stray chickens to run down.

One day Nan entered me into a children's beauty contest. This was to be my first experience of publicity and fame. I won the contest and my photo was in the local newspaper. My blond wavy hair, tanned skin, cheeky smile and sky blue eyes must have won over the judges. I wasn't a secret any more. I was out there in the world for all to see. I think that was the reason she entered me into that contest – a deliberate attempt to have me accepted into the community. Putting me out there, having me seen as a wonderful, beautiful child, just like other children. I had no idea that I was a bastard child with no father. It must have been a great relief for her, and just another wonderful magical day for me. But soon I would learn that with good days come bad days.

I was playing on my tricycle at the bottom of the garden; my safe, perfect little life was about to be shattered in a moment of learning – the first of many. As I pulled up on the front wheel, my trike flipped over backwards throwing me onto some broken concrete rocks with sharp flint stones sticking out from them, which struck the back of my head. The memory of the sharp cutting pain is still vivid.

I cried out for Nan and she came running down the garden. She pulled off her apron, rolling it up into a tight ball, pushed it hard into the back of my head, and then walked me up towards the house. The back door was open, and once inside she grabbed one of the big white towels, wrapping it awkwardly around my head. I was soon told that an ambulance had been called and was on its way. I am not sure I knew what an ambulance was, but it sounded reassuring and I felt sure that I would need to stop crying before it arrived. It seemed to be a forced cry of uncertainty, so it wasn't difficult for me to replace my crying with a brave sob. We were now at the front of the house on the public walkway – even more reason to stop crying. I stood there with Nan, waiting for the ambulance and trusting that all would be dealt with very soon. We watched for the ambulance together and soon it was there. It turned into the top of the road, cream coloured with a big red cross on its side, rapidly coming up to the house. Two men got out wearing dark blue uniforms and flat peaked hats. One removed the towel from my head, took a white bandage from his shoulder bag, and quickly wrapped the entire roll around my head before putting me into the back of the ambulance. Once inside, the two big doors were closed and off we went with bells ringing.

I don't remember what happened at the hospital, and I returned home having no idea of how long I had been away. All was strangely blank, but on my return I did notice that there was a new member of the household – a bright yellow canary. It was so beautiful, hopping from one side of the cage to the other. Nan would put the cage in direct sunlight by the back door. This would make the bird chirp and sing happily through the day. I was fascinated by its magical aliveness and its amazing carefree joy. I loved it, and wanted so much to hold it.

There were also pigeons in the chicken house shed that had not been there before. The pigeons were up high, I could barely see them, but I could hear them tooting and cooing. Who do they belong to, I wondered. Surely it had to be a man. I didn't remember seeing any men around the house, although many times I felt sure that someone else was around when I was sleeping at night. Did they come and go or did they live in the other bedroom? There was a second bedroom upstairs to the rear of the house that I was never allowed in; the door was always closed. I began to think that someone unknown to me lived in that room, but for some time yet they would remain unknown to me.

For now, I would stay close around the safety of my nan and the garden, but there was to be no tricycle any more. I had enjoyed my three-wheeler very much, but now it was gone and I did not understand why it had been taken away.

The freedom the tricycle had given me was short-lived and I was made to spend more time inside the house near my nan. Summer was nearing the end and autumn was on its way; I watched the leaves fall to the ground, leaving my giant trees bare to the sky. When winter came I spent a lot of time sitting up at the table with colouring book and pencils, colouring in with encouragement and guidance from Nan, sometimes becoming a little bored.

Often my attention would turn to the bright yellow canary. It was always busy doing something, moving about, hopping around, making noises. One day things seemed to be extremely quiet in the house, more quiet than normal. I had no idea where Nan had gone; she must have been upstairs making up the beds or something. I wanted to get closer to the canary so I pulled up a chair from the kitchen. Climbing up onto the chair allowed me to see directly into the cage; this was the first time I had been so close and alone with the little bird. I could see its tiny eyes and I wanted so much to hold it and touch it. I felt mesmerised by its beauty and I wanted to hold onto it. I felt like a cat just before it leaps at a bird. I had often watched the cat from next door staring at birds and stalking them in the garden. It was exciting watching as the cat tried to get close enough to pounce. I opened the cage door. I knew what I was doing was wrong, but I reached inside and grabbed the tiny bird tightly in my hand and took it from the cage. I kissed it on the head. The fluffy body felt so soft and delicate in my hand. Its eyes closed and it went still and motionless. I instantly knew that I had done something terribly wrong; I threw it to the floor. On hitting the floor, the bird immediately sprang back to life and flew towards the open door. It stopped on the doorstep.

My immediate feeling was of shock, I had no idea what I could do to reverse the situation. Then, out of nowhere, the cat from next door pounced onto the bird. I was horrified; I had made a big mistake. I jumped down from the chair and shouted, stamping my foot; the cat instantly released the bird. The cat also knew it had done wrong and darted off, hiding from sight. The bird lay motionless on the floor; its head hanging to one side. It was dead, and blood was coming from its bright yellow body. This was the first time I felt shame and guilt. I felt evil inside me. I was scared now and felt a strong need to hide. Where could I possibly hide? What have I done? The yellow bird was dead on the floor and I had killed it. Now I would be punished for it. What would Nan say to me? How could I explain what happened? I had no idea what to do. Maybe I could fix it, how can I fix it? I picked up the bird – it was warm, its blood was warm. But touching its blood scared me and I dropped it to the floor. I looked up towards the empty cage; the door was still open and the chair was still there. I needed to hide my connection with the killing. Maybe I could put the bird back into the cage. Yes, that's what I'll do. For a second time I picked up the dead bird, it felt horrible. I moved towards the chair.

At that moment my grandmother appeared.

"What have you done?" she asked.

She took hold of me tightly by the arm, the bird still in my hand. I was caught red-handed – I would always truly know the meaning of this phrase. The bird was put in the bin and my nan scrubbed my bloody hands, very hard, with soap and water.

"What have you done?" she kept saying over and over again, "It's Jack's bird." I had no idea who Jack was.

"The cat killed it," I said.

She didn't hear me. She dried my hands with a dirty rag, not a clean white towel as she would normally do. My hands still felt dirty. I was now a killer and the memory of killing something so beautiful haunted me for many years. Why had I done it? Did the cat kill the bird, or did I? I had nowhere to hide, so I would have to hide my shame and guilt inside me. I wanted to erase all that had gone before, but I couldn't. It was done. As the days passed and changed, so did I.

Sometime later, when it felt like the normality of daily life had returned, I was playing with a train set that my nan had laid out on the table for me when a man appeared and sat opposite me across the table. He stared at me with ice-blue eyes. He kicked my leg under the table and when I went to touch the train he aggressively pulled my hand away from it. I tried to pretend he wasn't there, tried to play on as if I hadn't noticed him. He continued to stare at me. I could see hate in his eyes. Why did he hate me? He kicked me again. Where was my nan? Who was this man? I was scared now. This must be Jack. It was his canary I had killed, and the pigeons must also belong to him. He snatched the train set away from me. The train set was his, and he was my uncle, the son of my grandmother. I sensed he would like to harm me, or maybe even kill me like I had killed his canary. My world of blissfulness and safety was shattered – I was not alone. There were other people in my perfect little world, who brought hostility, aggression and danger. I suddenly felt unsafe.

I was four years old now and things were changing around the house very fast. While I was getting bigger and stronger, I could see that Nan was becoming weaker with each day that passed. There was tiredness about her that I had not seen before, but still she would manage to take me to the park most days. One day she took me on the boating lake that we had passed so many times, but this time we hired a boat from the man in the boat shed. Nan gave him some money, he gave a ticket in return, helped us to get into one of the boats and then we were off. There were paddles on each side of the boat that needed to be turned by hand. It took us ages to complete the circuit around the island, stopping halfway around to have sandwiches and lemonade. I loved it. There were trees and bushes on the island that I longed to explore, but it was not allowed. One day in the future I would find my way onto the island, but for now it was all we could do to get back to where we had started. I did try to help Nan with the paddling and I proved to be just as inadequate as she was, but somehow together we managed it. I was very happy that day and enjoyed myself very much.

On the way home Nan took me to the railway bridge. The railway lines ran alongside the park and steam trains would pass by, belching out huge puffs of steam and smoke up into the air, up towards the clouds. Up onto the bridge we went, waiting for the next train to pass. I couldn't see over the walls of the bridge, but Nan stood there watching and waiting.

"Can you see the train, Nan?" I asked several times.

It wasn't long before she said, "There's one coming".

"Lift me up Nan, lift me up!"

"Wait a minute," she replied, "Come here, I will lift you up when the train comes." I stood waiting eagerly by her side.

"Nearly here ... ready and up we go!" She lifted me up and held me tight. "Hold on," she said. I gripped onto the top of the wall, helping her as I didn't want to slip down; I wanted to see the steam train for as long as possible. Nan wasn't very strong, and I am sure it was difficult for her to hold me.

Up I went and there it was, coming straight for me, a big steaming giant machine, like a monster, billowing out thick clouds of smoke and power.

"Woo, it's scary Nan!" I had never seen an engine before and now I was face to face with it. It seemed so amazingly powerful and unstoppable.

"What would it do to me, Nan?" I trusted my nan's knowledge and wisdom. Closer and closer it came, pumping out black clouds of steam and smoke.

"Hold on," she said and I did, and then it was there, right in my face. Be brave, I thought to myself, Nan's here with me, she knows what she's doing.

The clouds were all around us and then it was gone as quick as it came. Nan hurried to the other side as it went under the bridge, still holding me up so that I could see the full length of the train going away from us. It was a magical, powerful moment that I would never forget. That day was to be my last day out with her.

That night I snuggled up in my bed feeling safe and content, dreaming about what that day had brought to me. My world was changing around me and I was growing up into a boy. I had shared a wonderful day with Nan; she was all the world to me and I loved her dearly.

It seemed as if she knew our days together were coming to an end. She knew what was coming. Somehow I knew as well. I was sure she loved me and that she didn't have much time left for this world.

The days that followed would be my last at my grandmother's house. My uncle was around more often now, but I stayed well away from him. He had killed the cat from next door after he had caught it in his pigeon shed, and I was not allowed anywhere near his pigeons either. I was sure he hated me. I didn't feel safe when he was around.

As each day passed my nan seemed to spend more of her day lying down. She was getting weaker by the day. One day my uncle drew a picture of her in a coffin, a box for dead people. He showed it to her and she was clearly upset by it.

"You're wicked!" she said to him. He laughed. I didn't understand what was going on.

I wanted to make things better. I asked Nan if she would like to go to the park with me.

"No" she replied.

"Would you like some water?" I asked. 'No' again. I wondered if I could do anything for her. There seemed to be very little response. I feared she was going to die soon. I wondered who would look after me. How safe would I be?

There was this other woman now. She started coming to the house with a small child. The child was a girl, younger than myself. The woman told me that she was my mother and the girl was my sister. The woman was to be my new guardian, my real mother. The woman was the sister of my scary uncle. She seemed tense and stressed; she rushed around and was constantly on the move, always going somewhere. She was not calm like my grandmother.

"You're coming with me," she said one day, picking me up and putting me in the pram with my new sister, her at one end and me at the other.

"We're going to the shop," she said to my nan, "is there anything you need?" Nan didn't.

Off we went to the shops, much faster than I had ever gone before. I watched her face as we headed towards the shops; it looked tense. Down into the alleyway we went, my special alleyway where some years earlier I had left my body and seen all around. Three years had passed, three years of blissful growing up.

We were now in the high street and it was busy with people. I felt a sharp jolt as the pram dropped from the kerb into the road. I had felt the bump many times before when out with Nan, but the bump was never so alarming. It was a warning of what was to follow. There was a terrible screeching noise then a tremendous bang that lifted the pram off its wheels. The pram fell onto its side, throwing me onto the road. It had been struck by a car. My sister was still in the pram, strapped in. There were people running about in all directions, and screams and shouts as my sister was pulled from the pram. Someone picked me up from the road, but that's all I can remember. It was the last I saw of the pram.

We now had a new pushchair, which I think was a gift from the driver of the car. My new sister got to sit in the pushchair most of the time, meaning that I had to walk everywhere. One day I got to ride in the new pushchair alone, to the local shop, with my new mother. I think my sister was asleep at Nan's house. The shop was not in the main high street, it was a shop on its own in one of the side streets. It was a grocer's shop and sold just about everything. This was the first time I had felt any real connection with my mother. I can remember it all so clearly – it was dreamlike, very quiet, no sound. I remember the location. The front of the shop was all white with sunlight shining on it, making it seem very bright. There was strangeness, similar to the experience that I had years before whilst out in my pram with Nan, in the alleyway when I was up in the air looking down on myself. Yes, this was the same kind of feeling, seeing something that other people didn't see. So what was it that I was seeing now?

My new mother told me she going into the shop.

"I won't be long," she said, "you stay here in the sunshine".

Even though I remained sitting in the pushchair outside, I could see in my mind's eye what was happening in the shop. My mother and the shopkeeper had gone into the back room; I could see them having sex. My mother returned with three bags full of food.

We went back to my nan's house. My grandmother wasn't there; she had been taken to hospital. I spent a terrible and lonely night thinking about her, then the next morning my mother got me up and we were off again. This time we set off as a team, the three of us, my sister in the pushchair and me holding on, running alongside, almost being dragged along by my mother's speed. We were on our way to see Nan in hospital. She was dying of cancer and this would be the last time that I would see her. This day was about to turn my life inside out. This day was the beginning of a new life – a hard life. This day would leave me empty and bewildered. All that I had and all that I had known would be taken from me.

What I was left with was what I was dressed in – sandals, socks, grey shorts, a shirt and a jumper with no sleeves. A new mother, a new sister, and a new life of uncertainty. That day was to remain vivid for many years.

My last image of Nan was seeing her waving to me from the window of the hospital, her glasses on her face, no eyes for me to see. She blew a kiss and waved again. My new mother was with me, and my sister, but I felt that the kiss was for me. I still remember the window. I have passed it many times and looked, expecting to see her there waving to me, but I never saw her alive again.

I had been wonderfully sheltered for the first four years of my life. I had no idea how difficult it had been for my new mother and sister in their lives, so different from my own. But I was soon to learn. Many nights after Nan died were spent with my mother and sister and uncle sleeping in the park under the stars – the very same park that my grandmother had brought me to so often. I saw the stars in the sky for the very first time. I gazed up, staring deep into them and beyond, with longing. How bright they were. I felt certain that Nan had gone up there. That's where she was. I wanted to be with her. I called out to her in my mind.

"Where are you, Nan? I want to be with you. I want you to come back and get me. Why did you go and leave me here all alone? I need you. I don't feel safe any more and I'm scared. Please, please come back for me!"

There was no reply, just the endless unknowing of the stars and the darkness behind them. She was gone.

All was gone. Now I knew it, and understood that the person behind the glass windows would not be coming back. Everything had changed. I was here, stuck in this life, alone, and I would be alone for the rest of my life. I was cold and hungry and the ground was hard. The people I was with were strangers to me and I did not feel safe with them: my new mother and sister, my uncle who hated me, and my mother's boyfriend who I had not seen before. We had no home to go to. How could this be, and why? I couldn't understand it, but somehow I knew I needed to find a way to accept it.

I was devastated by this extreme change and would quietly struggle to recover from my loss. I missed my nan so much. I missed the walks to the parks with her, slow and gentle, with time to look at things, seeing them for what they really were. When I got cold and tired I would close my eyes and see us snuggled up together in her chair, warm in front of the fire. I could see her and feel her, and sometimes I could smell her. This kept me warm inside.

But however much I tried to comfort myself, the sudden change in my life was to have a profound and lasting effect on me; I would never feel safe again.

Summer had gone and winter was on its way again. It was time for me to grow up and learn how to be someone else. We would be homeless for that winter; we slept in different parks at night and sometimes even in the toilets. The toilets were often left open at night; my mum's boyfriend had spoken to the park attendant, making arrangements for them to be left open. At least we were dry and out of the wind. Sometimes we would sleep at different houses, on the floor or sofa or even a bed with something to eat. Winter came and went and it was not long before winter returned again. I had no idea where summer had gone.

Soon we would learn that the local church was responsible for getting us a temporary home for the winter, which proved to be a very cold one. We were to move in before Christmas, but it was no hotel. There were broken windows, no heating, no hot water, no bath, and the toilet was outside, broken and dirty. The floors were bare with no coverings. It was very cold and dark inside, derelict and empty – nothing! But at least it was inside and we could stay there for the coming winter.

My mother's boyfriend scrubbed the place from one end to the other with disinfectant and hot water, boiled in a pot on the stove. He fixed the windows and covered the holes in the floor with a kind of vinyl lino. It wasn't very warm but it was clean and it kept the draughts out.

Maybe life would be different now.

Chapter 2

I am five years old and life is cold, dark, hard and scary with memories that haunt me. One night when woken from a deep warm sleep, with darkness all around, I found myself in a large bed; I had no idea whose bed it was, I didn't care, I was tired and wanted to sleep. My mother came to the bed followed by a man, a stranger unknown to me. My mother entered the bed at my end and the man entered at the other end.

I remained motionless and silent, then drifted back into sleep. I was awoken later by movement in the bed. They were locked together, I could feel them thrusting uncontrollably as they lunged into each other. I was caught in a moment, unable to move or speak; I had no idea of what I should do. A feeling of silent fear and rage took over my body. My heart was pounding; it felt like I was about to die. I wanted the feelings inside me to stop. The two in the bed showed little regard for me, and a deep anger lodged itself into my body. My warm safe place was shattered, taken from me. I needed somehow to escape from my feelings and get out of my body, but I was unable to move, struck dumb and trapped. In a nightmare I could not escape from. What was I to do?

I floated down, deep inside me, searching for myself, searching for a power greater than myself. This something inside me I came to know as my angel. My angel would look after me for many years to come, never being far away. She would advise me, tell me things and give me comfort, always letting me know that I was safe and not alone.

"Please help me, Angel," I called out into my mind, "Take me away from here!"

In a flash I was gone, removed from what was going on. When morning came, I had no recall of what had gone before. I had emptied my mind and discarded all memories of that night, hiding them away for many years.

That was my first encounter with the harsh reality of my mother's physical activities with men. My relationship with her would never recover. The seed had been planted and the damage was done. She had no idea of my needs; I had to learn how to look after myself.

We were now living in our new house and were almost like a family, my mother, my sister and my mother's regular boyfriend, Alfie. To start with the small stove was used for cooking and boiling hot water, but slowly things improved. A tin bath appeared which we would bath in once a week, it was hung on the wall when not in use; and we had a gas stove to cook on. This was home now, my new home, inside away from onlookers. We didn't have to hide any more. This would be a new start for us. Alfie was working and kept saying that he was going to buy a car. We settled in. My new sister and I had a single bed each in the upstairs room at the front of the house. It looked out onto the road; across the road was a school for very young children. The school would become a place of safety for me, a place that I could escape to for a while.

In front of the window was a high bush that stopped the sunlight coming in. The bush made noises at night when the wind blew, scratching at the glass, and would cast scary shadows onto the walls that moved around the room, silhouetted by the passing lights of vehicles and the street lamps outside. It was a scary room, always dark, cold and empty.

Alfie seemed a good man. He went out to work early each morning, lighting the wood-burning stove before leaving. I would get up close to the fire in order to get warm while eating my bowl of porridge. It was always porridge with sugar in the winter, and cornflakes with water in the summer. I soon learned to boil an egg in a saucepan, two minutes for soft and three minutes for hard. Alfie taught me. My mother had no idea how to cook anything. Cooking held no interest for her.

It was Alfie, not my mum, who treated me and my sister for the head lice that plagued us. This was another source of shame: I hated the idea of having living bugs in my hair, and felt anxious and panicky as he rubbed on the liquid to treat it then combed out the lice with a fine metal toothcomb.

We live on a diet of beans on toast, egg on toast, jam on toast, porridge with sugar, and bread and sugar sandwiches. When there was nothing else Alfie told me to always eat bread with my porridge – "That will stop you feeling hungry," he said, and it did – also broken biscuits and stale cakes from the bakers when things got short towards the end of the week. Dripping and bread, the dripping was left over from the weekend if we were lucky enough to have meat. Sunday was the only day we had a cooked dinner, cooked by Alfie. This would always be potatoes, cabbage, mince and Yorkshire puddings with gravy. And water from the cabbage was Alfie's speciality with salt and pepper; he always encouraged me to drink it, I loved it. He said it would keep me fit and healthy, I was sure it did. We never ate at a table, maybe because there wasn't one; like wild animals we would come in some kind of pecking order and then take food off in different directions to preferred places of solitude to eat.

It wasn't long before it was necessary for me to attend a dentist for treatment and removal of decayed teeth. Too much sugar and lack of good, healthy food. Food, or the lack of it, was to be an on-going problem for some time to come, but Christmas was a period of abundance. More food than we could eat, lasting for days, possibly a couple of weeks.

Christmas is almost here. It was the first time I had celebrated Christmas with my mother and it seemed to be of special importance to her. She made many demands on Alfie and would often scream and shout at him, calling him names if he failed to meet her demands. When she was angry she had a vicious manner of name calling, screaming, swearing and shouting words of threat and abuse. She was intimidated by no one and no matter how good things seemed, she would always bring things crashing down, raging over the need for more money.

On more than one occasion I remember my mother calling me 'the child from the sky'. Then she would laugh, and I had no idea why; as time passed I was to gain some understanding of what she meant by it.

Soon I was to attend the school that was across the

road. My first day arrived; I had looked forward to this for some time. The sound of the children woke me every morning, their shouts and screams of joy filling me with longing. From my bedroom window I had a full view of their play times, the children playing, running from one side of the playground to the other. I was so excited at the thought of being with them, being part of real life. I wanted so much to escape my harsh existence in our broken down house and grab hold of the life on offer in the school opposite.

My bedroom was much brighter now, a brightness which I had not previously noticed. The bushes had been cut shorter allowing the blue sky and sunlight to shine into the room. I was up, dressed and ready to go. Then Alfie came into my bedroom, unexpected and clearly troubled in some way. Why was he not at work? He seemed angry and annoyed with me in a way that I had not felt or seen in him before now. He was angry that I hadn't tied my shoelaces. He knelt down to tie them, which put his head very close to me, just a few inches from my eyes; I felt as if I could see into his head and read his thoughts. Then I understood that it wasn't me he was angry with, but my mother. She had not come home last night – she was out all night.

I could feel his pain and stress. He tied my shoelaces quickly and aggressively. I felt sorry for him, but also wondered if this would stop me going to school. I could see that he was faced with a problem – his immediate problem was me! This was my special day, going to school with the children across the road, inside the school gates, the day I had been longing for now for many weeks. I could feel my excitement draining out of my body. As I sensed the seriousness of his problems, sadness and doubt began to replace my previous enthusiasm. Then I sensed that Alfie was going to deal with the problem in a positive way, just as he had so many times before; I somehow knew that I would be OK and would get to school. I also remembered that he had been starting a new job that morning and realised he must have already been to his new job and returned back home. I felt admiration for him, but was also anxious about what I'd come home to.

Alfie took me to school and left me at the side door where a woman teacher was waiting. He told her my name, Stephan Chadwick, and she wrote it on the tag she held and then she took hold of my hand reassuringly. "Go inside, Stephan," she said.

Alfie then turned and walked away and I wondered if I would ever see him again, but I sensed that he was relieved to know that I was safe and no longer a problem for him.

It was cosy and warm inside. It felt safe like Nan's house. What a wonderful feeling it was for me. It gave me tremendous hope – all was not lost! I was now happy and excited again, but I didn't say much. I was very quiet, always looking, watching movement and activity around me, always very aware, seeing things that were happening around me, always thinking. My eyes were my first line of defence, always gathering information. I needed to see the world and to try to understand people if I was to learn, if I was to survive the complexity of my circumstances. I had to open my mind so that I might find safety and stability.

It was not long before I received a hug from one of the female teachers. There were three or four women in the room and they made me feel safe and loved. How I longed to feel safe and loved. I had no idea that my soul was screaming out for love, to feel safe. How I longed for their hugs. I was aware of how warm, soft and gentle the women were, so different from my mother. I remember one lady squeezing me and cuddling me into her big warm breasts, the softness of her jumper, the clean sweet smell of her body and clothes. I fell into her and for a moment I was hopelessly lost in her and I wanted her never to let go of me. I clung onto her, fearful she would leave me.

She had found my open wound unguarded. I felt a kind of shame and fear growing in me. There was a screaming inside me that made no sound, which could not be heard or seen. I was fearful that she would see how much I needed her. Please don't let go of me, I thought. I felt that I would cry. I must not cry! I must not show how vulnerable and sensitive I am. I must hide this terrible fear that I have inside me.

I wanted her to take me home – to her home, not to mine! I fell in love with her and I did not want her to leave me. I did not want to be alone, ever again. I felt sad and vulnerable, overwhelmed. I said nothing as she lowered me down to the floor, and then she let me go and she was gone. I never ever saw her again. It was like when Nan died; it hurt me and left an empty space inside me. At that moment in my tiny mind and body I became fully aware for the first time how damaged, vulnerable and insecure I was, needing so much to feel safe and loved, to belong somewhere with a grown-up person that I could trust to take care of me. I was so scared now and I didn't want to feel myself being so needy. I had to protect myself even more now. It was so overwhelming and painful, too much for me to understand. I needed not to feel my feelings. I had to be strong, and detached! Detachment was to become a necessity for my daily survival.

What happened that day put me in two worlds. One was the school across the road from home. That world was warm and safe, full of joy and fun, but somehow unreal to me. My other world was a place of reality that I would have to return to after school. That place was cold and hard, dirty, a place where I felt alone, a place where I slept in a cold, dark room with a sister, Marie, who never spoke. She was also alone in that cold, dark room listening to my mother's screaming and shouting. Each night I held on to my dreams of tomorrow, when I could escape again from the cruel, cold, empty harshness of this house across the road and behind the school gates.

I grew to love school and the softness of the sweet-smelling teachers who would hug me. There were beds in a side room and every day the children would get to sleep in the beds. We were made to sleep in silence for a period of time, which to me seemed endless. I had no idea how long it was, it seemed like a whole lifetime. It was wonderful. I was able to escape into a place where I was able to feel safe and warm, no fear and no cares, a place I remembered from long ago, a place of light, a place of love, no danger. The same place my angel came from, or was it just Nan's house I could remember?

After some weeks it seemed that in some way I was set aside from the other children. I was not quite sure why, but seemingly I was creative and artistic in the tasks given me to complete, always being positive and eager to do well. I was openly liked and often I would be told how clever I was, hugs included, which encouraged me to be even more clever. I was doing joined up writing before any of the other children, reading just as well as any other child and enjoying it very much. It gave me a feeling of belonging and I had a sense of who I might be.

Several times I was sent along with my work to the headteacher. She seemed to like me very much, in fact I felt loved, unconditionally loved! How lucky I felt. She was a good-looking woman, not in the same way as my mother who looked like a film star, hard and cold, false, unapproachable. This woman was real – handsome, gentle and soft, elegant and dignified, alive, warm and loving. She was a real woman, a real human person who knew how to love. I couldn't help wondering if the other children received as much warmth and love from her as I did. Did they even go to her room, I wondered. She would call me to her, sit me on her knee and chat with me for a while, though I said little in return. She was so bubbly, happy and dynamic, with a sense of magical power about her. How I wished she could be my mum. She would question me about things at home, but I made little or no reply.

I later found out that I had suffered from selective mutism: not speaking when spoken to, not knowing what to say, thinking about the question asked of me rather than thinking about what to reply – over-thinking, pondering what the truth might be and the true meaning of words. By the time all this thinking and analysing had taken place it seemed pointless to reply. I think the real reason for her questions was related to her concern for my home life. She could see my house from her office window, just over there, across the road, my other world, my real world – cold and dirty, empty, devoid of love. That was the place where I slept until tomorrow, when I would return to school again, which was safe and warm, where I was truly loved. This is the place where I belong. This is the place where I grow and learn. This is the place where I get strong and find a sense of who I am. This is the place where I want to be. This is where I know the truth of people's love. This is the place where I will not be abandoned. This is the place where I will not be alone. This is the place where I am unafraid. This is the place where I am loved. This is the place for me. I shall return tomorrow and the next day. I will never stop coming back until I need come back no more, until I have felt all the love that I am able to feel. I will keep coming back until I am fully healed, until I am unafraid, until I have no more pain.

But the truth is, school was only a small part of my life, just for a few hours each day, and then at the end of each day I would be alone again, having to make decisions and suppress my fears and feelings. Once I had crossed the road I would need to find a way to sneak into the house, unnoticed if possible. I hated going home! I knew she would be waiting. That morning I had sneaked away from her. She had wanted me to stay home from school. Many times she told me how desperately she needed me to stay home, sometimes offering me money. This was to become a regular demand. She would blame me for her daily problems. She said she needed to go out here and there for a few hours and would I look after Marie. I would feel disloyal and guilty, but I needed to be at school – it was all I had.

Things between me and my mother were not always so bad. Some days she would take me out with her. On one such day she took me into the city on the tube, the underground train – so called, I supposed, because it travelled underground. Outside the windows I saw dark tunnels. These tunnels went deep underground, under the roads, the houses and the large, high buildings all across the great city of London. It was a little scary at first, but then I found it very exciting – there was a big, magical world out there for me to find and explore.

We were met at the central London station by a man. I was sure that I had seen him somewhere before. I was very clean and smart looking that day, with new clothes. My mother looked like a film star, wearing big dark glasses. She was a good-looking woman. From the station we took a black taxi – I had never seen one before. It all felt so special. The taxi took us to a large block of apartments, passing the palace where the Queen lived. There were soldiers outside in red coats. I was excited. The sky was blue and the sun was shining – it felt good to be alive. I was happy.

The man who met us was clearly wealthy and seemed to be a person of some importance. He gave me some money and when he smiled I could see that he had one or two gold teeth, which impressed me. The man spoke with what I thought was an Italian accent and my mother confirmed this by telling me that he was from Italy. His apartment was extremely luxurious. To my amazement, at one end of the main room there was a huge cage, which stretched from one side of the room to the other, and inside was a large monkey. The man said that if I wanted to, I could feed it a banana. It looked scary to me and I shook my head from side to side, hoping that he would accept my refusal as final. There was some talk between my mother and the man. They then explained to me that I would be left alone for a short time and they would be in an adjacent room. I heard the lock turn in the door. It was probably twenty to thirty minutes before they were to return. I never saw the man or the monkey again.

Several times while I was out with her I would be left alone in a small park somewhere close to a tube station. She would give me money and tell me to wait there and not to wander off.

"I'll be back soon," she would say, "I've just got to see someone and I won't be very long."

I had no idea where she went. I didn't really want to know. On one occasion it seemed like hours; I thought she had forgotten me and would never return. I started doubting her promises and became aware that I might be in some kind of danger. I could feel how vulnerable I was, powerless and small, unable to protect myself against the world around me and from this woman, my guardian. The thoughts were daunting and during those times alone I increasingly felt the need to stay in close touch with my true guardian – my angel, never far away!

I now had two sisters. It seemed as though a new one had appeared out of nowhere. This gave my mother even more reason to keep me home from school. I had to learn how to look after my new sister and change her nappies when needed. This was to become one of my regular duties. I soon got the hang of it, but when I got the chance I was off and away from the house, across the road through the magic gates where I was safe from my mother. I knew she would not come looking for me at school. She was too ashamed. She had no power over me there. I was safe there, but always had to return home at the end of the school day.

I dreaded the long nights. The cold dark emptiness of lonely thoughts constantly filled my head, floating out and up, entwining with the cold dark air and then out through the window into the darkness of night. I could always see the stars in my mind and beyond. Back in the room, my sister Marie was over in the corner. I could not see her, but I knew she was there, even though there was no movement, no sound. Often I wanted so much to go to her and speak with her, but I never did, it didn't seem possible. I didn't know her and I didn't know how to reach out to her. I had no idea what she was feeling inside. I never saw any signs of emotion come from her. What would I say to her if I could? How would I tell her that I felt concern for her and that I wanted to love her and protect her, but that I had no idea how I could possibly do so? I recognised a strength in her that I knew so well, detachment from reality and emotions in order to survive one's true feelings and needs.

I was woken by the shouts and screams of my mother coming through the wall. I stared into the cold, dark air, the broken glass in the window pierced by the streetlights. I was not afraid, but I was shocked and shaken, and my body shuddered uncontrollably at the sound of her screams as they came through the wall like sharp spears striking deep into my body.

"You fucking German bastard," she screamed out, followed by crash that shook the wall. I curled up under my blankets like a tiny hedgehog imagining that I had spikes sticking out from me that would protect me from her screaming, ugly, raging voice. I was cold and I felt sad. I almost wanted to cry, but I knew that crying would not help. She continued to scream and shout, and the sounds continued to pass through the wall. I heard the shrieks of her terrible voice and I hated her even more.

I could hear no response from Alfie. I could not understand why he did not respond. I wanted him to hit her, to beat her. I wanted him to stop her terrible screams and her ugly shouts of violence. I wanted him to smash her horrible mouth so she could no longer shout. I wanted him to kill her.

In my mind I called out into the darkness, "Please stop, please stop." I called out to my angel, "Please Angel, please stop her shouting. Where is my Nan, why did she have to go and die? Why did she leave me here alone? I'm so scared, I need her to come back, please ask her to come and take me away from here. I don't want to be here. I want that terrible woman to die. Take me away from this terrible place."

My angel came to the side of the bed and spoke to me,
"Your grandmother is unable to come back, but she will always be with you and she will always love you, as I do,

and remember I will always be here with you. When you need me I will come to you and I will look after you. There is no need to be afraid. I am never far from you. I am in you and I always know and feel your pain and your fears."

Then my angel was gone.

My angel always made me feel safe and reassured. She would return to me many times in the future when I truly needed her, saving my life in later years when it was in danger.

The days seemed to pass with some kind of routine, but the truth was there was no routine, no normality! Every day was an unknown event. Nothing was certain except the uncertainty. I had hoped to build some kind of bond with my mother, but this proved to be impossible, as I had come to truly hate and despise her. We had become enemies, but she was all I had; I was at her mercy. I had to somehow find a way to adjust into this new life. What was it that I needed to do in order that daily life would be more acceptable, without fear or struggle? I tried cleaning the house and occasionally stayed home from school to look after my new sister as best I could, and sometimes I got paid money for my willingness.

Christmas was almost here and this gave some sense of bonding between us as a family. I felt there was a role for me to play of some importance and responsibility. Alfie had become my dad now, he had adopted me and I had now his surname, Sims. He was a good man, always busy doing something around the house, and when he wasn't at home he was out at work earning money to bring home to my mother. Often she would go to his job on payday to collect the money. I would guard the house and look after my sisters.

Sometimes my mother would not return home until long after Alfie had arrived home from work; sometimes with food and shopping, and sometimes without. Marie was very capable of looking after herself, but unavailable to me and to everyone else, just as I was to them. Alfie, unknown to me at the time, was a gambling man. Maybe that was the reason my mother went to his place of work to collect his wages on a Friday. Come Monday all the money was gone and we would go hungry until next payday.

One of the most important jobs was to keep the stove burning throughout the winter. Anything that would burn would go into the fire, old unusable shoes, papers, wood and rubbish. It was easy enough, drop the front cover plate and put in all that was available. I enjoyed cleaning up around the house. It gave me a feeling of wellbeing. My belief was that if I could keep the house clean then things would change for the better.

My mother was always happy when she had money to spend, but it didn't last very long. I would often be sent with an unreadable begging note to the local shops for food. I soon became well known to the shopkeepers. They always found it difficult to read my mother's list of requirements and her promises to pay them back at the weekend; she was no good at spelling. I became popular with the shopkeepers, always returning home with food. They seemed to like me as much as the teachers did at school. I didn't really like begging for food, having no money, handing over a tiny piece of scrap paper with unreadable words on it, often taking at least two people to understand it, but I was sure they were always as happy and pleased to see me as I was to see them. I would get broken biscuits and stale cakes from the bakers and I soon learned how to keep some of the food for myself, hiding my rewards outside the house, returning later to collect my valued treasure and go back to my bedroom to eat in secrecy in the darkness, sometimes sharing with my sisters.

I crossed the road to school every day without any problems, but up towards the shops there was a bend in the road that was a blind spot for vehicles. I would sometimes call in at the greengrocer's that was on that bend. The two ladies there were always pleased to see me, giving me some fruit to take home. I was very fond of apples and bananas.

"You be careful crossing that road," they would always call out to me on leaving.

"Yes," I would reply, "Thank you."

Crossing on the bend meant that I would have to run harder and faster across the road, which I always did, not being able to see any approaching vehicles fully. One day I took the risk and made a run for it. When crossing I saw from the corner of my eye a motorbike heading straight at me, which I had not expected. I could see a man and a woman on the bike wearing crash helmets and goggles. I looked directly into their eyes and could see the terror in their faces just as they took off into the air over my head, followed by the motorbike, which landed inches from me. I could sense their fear of killing me, a small child.

I did not stop. I kept running until I reached home. I had done something terribly wrong; surely they would come looking for me. I feared that the two people were dead or seriously injured or damaged in some way. I needed to hide. I went to my bedroom and got into bed, burrowing under the blankets. My heart was pounding and I was so scared, more scared than I had ever been before. This was a different kind of fear; I had no idea what I should do. I could hear people calling and shouting, and then there was banging at the front door and the back door. What was I to do?

I somehow managed to open the door, not really wanting to. There were policemen there and a doctor, and all sorts of people appearing from nowhere.
"Where is your mum?" they kept asking me. I had no idea where she was, out as always.

The doctor said that I was in shock and needed to go to hospital, and soon I was taken off in an ambulance. I was later told by a doctor at the hospital that the two people were not seriously injured as they were lucky enough to have landed in a field of deep grass, but their bike was beyond repair. I felt ashamed of myself and sorry for the man and woman. I could still see the terror in their eyes behind the glass goggles. I had seen it, and I had felt it deep inside me. Where did these feelings come from? Sometimes the intensity of my feelings became too much for me, but I had no way of telling anyone – and to me it was all a normal part of living and learning.

I never crossed the road again at the bend, but I still

had to cross the road every day. Daily risks and daily dangers seemed to become part of normal life.

My next scrape with danger was on a cold, frosty winter morning, just before Christmas. A motorbike again, this time it had three wheels instead of two, with a side-box. The bike came out from the factories at the back of our house. There was an archway between our house and the next one, with a track that gave access to vehicles from the main road to the factories at the bottom of our garden. This time I was on a tricycle. I could hear the motorbike coming through the archway, but as I had no brakes I kept peddling as fast as I could, trying to cross before it came out from the archway. I ran straight into it – the gear lever struck me under the armpit, making a hole; my left hand was burnt on the exhaust pipe. Once again I was taken off to hospital in an ambulance.

I was beginning to learn that each day was different from the one before; each day was a new day, an unknown adventure, with unknown possibilities. There was no certainty as to what that day may bring. All things in that day were unknown, undecided. I found this quite exciting – the unknowingness of life, all things constantly changing and out of control. I became aware of the tremendous freedom that I had, and the magic of every day. Perhaps it was me that was out of control and constantly changing. I was left free to run wild. I was unkempt, received no guidance or advice. The risky magic of everyday life was to be my teacher and I felt no fear of it. But I was in need of a new bike, again – maybe I would get one for Christmas.

Christmas was here and paper decorations were being made and hung on the walls and ceiling by Alfie. Marie and I helped by licking and sticking coloured strips of paper together, which made up long lengths of paper chains that hung down from the ceiling and walls. It all looked pretty and colourful and I was excited at the possibility of things to come. There was lots of food in the house, more food than I had ever seen before. Alfie would always bring home lots of food and things on Christmas Eve.

Bedtime came very late, Marie and I were assured that Father Christmas would be coming that very night and he would somehow manage to come down the chimney. I didn't understand why he needed to come down the chimney carrying sacks of presents, leaving his sledge and reindeer's parked on the roof. It didn't seem like a good idea – why couldn't we leave the back door open for him? My sister and I waited, and waited. We listened for movement and sounds from the chimney. I looked out from the window. The sky outside was dark; there was snow on the rooftops but no sign of reindeers pulling sledges across the sky. Outside became darker and darker, and soon my sister was sleeping. I lay there thinking and looking at the empty fireplace. I was sure that he would come soon, but I found it difficult to stay awake.

I slept the whole night through until early morning, awakening with excitement and great expectation. Yes, he had been as promised, presents all around. Boxes wrapped in brightly coloured Christmas paper. Such excitement I had not felt before. I leapt out of bed, the cold air having no effect on my ability to tear open the boxes marked with my name. What a day! As much as we could possibly want to eat in one day, and much more in the days to follow. The stove in the kitchen was fully stacked with red glowing coke, a type of coal that lasted longer. The kitchen was very warm, much warmer than I had known it before. There was the table, now covered with fruit, cakes and biscuits and much more. My mother was still sleeping in bed. Alfie soon went back to bed with her. He said that he had waited up all night for Santa and now he needed to get some sleep. The day seemed to go on forever. There was no screaming, no shouting and we were warm, loads of food, and gifts to open and play with through the day. I felt content and for the first time I could feel a safeness in the house. I so much wanted it to last. By the end of the day I was exhausted and tired, looking forward to sleeping in my bed.

Before bedtime came I gathered together all the presents I had received that day. A space suit that was to become my daily protection from the world. That suit was very special to me, it enabled me to separate from the world and be in it at the same time. I felt Father Christmas must have known what he was doing. A jet plane with a real engine. I was told that it was very expensive and it could really fly up into the sky. I was sure that it had come from one of my mother's rich boyfriends; the giver was kept a secret. A set of carpenter's tools that I constantly used around the house, repairing all that I could find. In the two weeks of Christmas I had almost rebuilt the house. My most treasured gift was a Meccano set, bought by my Uncle Jack whose canary I had killed when living at my grandma's house. He must have forgiven me.

The Meccano set opened my creative mind to many ideas. I would spend many hours and days building structures and mechanical moving cranes and bridges. This enabled me to lose myself in a magical world of creative ideas. I loved it and knew from the special feeling I got from my creations that my mind was capable of reaching out beyond the difficulties of daily life. I was able to escape, building and creating things with my Meccano set.

Christmas soon passed and life returned to the usual uncertainty, but now my gifts would help me through the coming days. Days when not at school would be spent babysitting and cleaning, tidying up around the house. On some occasions I even resorted to scrubbing the lino floors that Alfie had put down. I had watched him clean the floors several times in the past. I wanted to please him and make him proud of me. I wanted to form a bond with him. I saw that he was consistent, determined and resourceful, always cooking the Sunday dinner – our only cooked dinner each week. I was always hungry; I had to search for food and come up with ideas, using whatever could be found. Beans on toast or egg on toast was a luxury, bread and butter with jam was a treat, and cheese was rare. Sometimes I would boil myself an egg and put it between two slices of bread with lots of salt on top. Once the bread was gone I knew I would be taking a trip to the shops with a begging note.

My mother had no idea of how to cook anything. I found it hard to see or feel any true usefulness in her. I felt nothing from her. She constantly failed to care for our basic needs. Truth is she didn't know how. I think that she was deeply troubled, mixed up in her head and uncertain of the future. I don't think she knew what she wanted. Her father and mother had died, she had been homeless, unmarried, no income and expecting another child. She had nothing but her looks and vicious temper. She was very lucky to have Alfie, with all the qualities that he had, but still life must have been very difficult for both of them. It was lucky that Alfie had been willing to take on a child that wasn't his. I was sure she had very little love for him. I suppose that made it even more difficult for her. She said to me, "One day, when you get older, you will understand."

My mother calls.

"Take your sister with you to the bus stop and meet your dad," she commanded.

What bus stop? Why does she want us gone?

"The bus stop is the one past the Sunday School Church. Go on, off you go," she commands again. I had no idea where the Sunday School Church was.

"Wait for him at the bus stop."

Off I went, my sister refusing to hold my hand or do anything I asked of her, as usual. We waited forever at the bus stop. Buses came and went but no sign of our dad. A man came and spoke to us.

"Hello," he said, "are you alone?" I made no reply; he seemed more interested in my sister than me.

She answered him. "We are waiting for our dad."

"Are you sure you haven't missed him? What does he look like?" he asked.

No reply.

"Are you sure you haven't missed him? Where do you live?" he asked.

"By the school," I said.

"I am sure I saw him walking that way," he said, "Come on, let's go and find him."

This made me confused. Maybe we had missed him. He took hold of my sister's hand and tried to take hold of mine, but I refused.

"Come on, let's go and find him. I will take you home."

My feelings were confused. I was unsure of him. He smiled at us. He was clean and well dressed. It seemed that his intentions might well be good. I had no idea what I was supposed to do.

He walked on with my sister, which required me to follow. He seemed concerned for our safety. He told us that he was going to buy us an ice cream, which left me in no doubt of his good intentions, and at least we were heading in the direction of home, which I found reassuring. We came to the Sunday School church, which was about halfway home.

"Have you ever been in the church?" he said.

"No," my sister replied. I wasn't even asked.

"Come on, I will show you around," and off he went through the gates and into the grounds of the church, giving me little choice but to follow. The man led us around to the back of the church; he seemed to know where he was going.

"When will we get an ice cream?" my sister asked.

"Soon," he replied.

I was beginning to feel uneasy and afraid of the situation. He seemed to change and became anxious. There was a shed at the back. He tried to take my sister inside and told me to wait outside.

"Pretend we are at the doctor's surgery," he said, "You just wait there for your turn. I won't be long."

"I'm going home," I said, "Come out, Marie!"

"She's OK, don't worry," he said, "I am a doctor. She won't be too long. Be a good boy and wait there for your sister."

I pulled at my sister's arms, calling for her to come with me.

"I am going home to get my uncle!" I shouted out. I had no idea what was going on but I didn't like it and sensed that we were in danger.

"It's OK," he said again, "I'm going to get you an ice cream now for being such good children. You wait here for me. I won't be long." And off he went.

"Are you OK?" I asked my sister. She made no reply.

"Come on," I said, "we need to get home."

"I want to wait for my ice cream."

"You can't, you've got to come home with me."

"No, I am not!" she insisted.

I grabbed her arm again and started pulling at her. She refused to come. We waited, ten minutes passed.

"He won't come back" I said to her, "Come on, let's go home. Dad will be at home now and maybe he will buy an ice cream for us."

She quickly changed her mind and we walked home together. I think we were both very lucky not to have been harmed that day. This would not be the last time a man would try to take my sister.

We returned home to find no one there. They were out looking for us. That night I had a sense that I had failed: the world was dangerous and as a child I was powerless to do anything about it. I understood that some people were good and some people were evil, but how was I supposed to know which ones were evil?

One day the police came to the house, looking for stolen goods. My stepdad told the officer, "Have a look around, you won't find very much here. Look in the larder. That's the food cupboard there, have a look inside. You won't find any food there."
I was looking at the policemen's faces. I saw their eyes looking around the room for confirmation of what was being said. They seemed assured that they would find very little and searching would prove to be a waste of time.
"OK," they said, "we'll leave you to get on. Sorry to have bothered you." And they went about their business.
To my surprise, the larder was packed tight with boxes and boxes of food that my dad had stolen from a shop whilst doing some painting work there.

On foggy nights my mother would go out with a friend stealing clean washing from clothes lines hung up in people's gardens. A pram was used to bring the washing home. They would only take the most expensive garments – sheets, towels and such like.

If it wasn't the local police calling at the house, it was the military police looking for my uncle who had gone missing from the army. National Service they called it. Two big guys wearing steel like helmets. They searched everywhere for him, under my bed, under the floorboards, in the larder now empty of food once more, as normal. They left, but said they would be back. I never saw them again. I didn't see my uncle either. Maybe they had caught up with him.

This all seemed to be normal daily activity. Alfie kept on working, bringing money home for my mother, and soon he would have a delivery job. This job came with a van full of cakes, which he often brought home. Sometimes he took me out with him in the van, on orders from my mum who was always trying to get rid of me when I wasn't needed to look after my sisters. The only problem was that I would have to sit in the back, surrounded by wasps crazy for sweet-smelling jam and sugar doughnuts. I soon learned that cakes came with wasps and there would always be at least half a dozen wasps in there at any time. I never did get stung; I was willing to put up with them, and it soon became clear they were more interested in the jam than me! I loved it in the van. I used to pretend I was a large doughnut and enjoyed the sense of danger with the unpredictable wasps hovering around. After making deliveries to the local baker's shops, my stepdad would drop me back home with a large bag of jam doughnuts to share with my sisters, Marie and Laine, before returning to the place where he worked.

My stepdad was soon to get his own car. Wow, what a change it made to our lives! I could see he was proud of it. It made him happy and surer of himself and, more importantly, it had a positive effect on my mother. Friday nights became regular trips out in the car to the fish and chip shop in town. Friday night was also pay night, which meant money to spend and food to eat. There was always a queue of people at the fish shop, so we would have to wait in the car while Alfie queued for our supper. I would sit in the driver's seat grasping the steering wheel with both hands. I would stand on the seat to see out of the window and imagine myself driving the car along the street. I always looked forward to Friday nights when Alfie would arrive home and then the drive to town to collect our fish and chips. White fish in golden batter, salt and lots of vinegar.

After catching me in the driving seat once or twice, Alfie took to sitting me on his lap whilst driving home and I would get to hold onto the steering wheel. Alfie always made me feel that things in life were good and positive. I liked him and I didn't understand why he wasn't my real dad. He was a good man. He did all he could to meet my mother's constant demands, but it proved never to be enough.

I learned he served in the Royal Navy during the war with Germany. He was a young man of only 17 or 18 years of age and received five war medals. His skipper was Lieutenant-Commander Peter Scott, son of the famous Scott of the Antarctic, well known for his attempt to reach the South Pole. Scott and his brave team died in their attempt, and no one came back alive. Peter Scott was distinguished for carrying out many search and destroy missions against the German navy in the Mediterranean Sea and the Atlantic Ocean, operating in small fast torpedo boats in which Alfie was a crew member.

Alfie was a gunner and sometimes he would tell me stories about their search and destroy raids on German and Italian war ships in the Mediterranean Sea. The boats were made of lightweight plywood, fully loaded with petrol and six high explosive torpedoes, with two large petrol engines capable of very high speeds. One tiny spark would cause the boat to explode, it sounded very dangerous to me. Alfie once told me about a night when he was on watch, looking out to sea with pair of binoculars. On resting his eyes and looking down to the sea at the side of their boat he spotted a mine just a few feet away. He explained that because it was so close he was doubtful about calling out, feeling guilty and responsible for not spotting the mine sooner. He decided that the honourable thing to do was to push the mine as far away from the boat as he could before calling out a warning to the skipper. It was a very scary and dangerous situation, and he was concerned that a sudden warning might cause confusion and panic, resulting in the boat accelerating in the wrong direction. So saying nothing, he pushed the mine away with a boarding pole before calling out. I understood how he must have felt. I was proud of him and this gave me a sense of pride and well being.

The following Christmas Alfie gave me his five medals in a box. I saw something in his eyes that I didn't quite understand. Why was he giving them to me? Surely he was proud of them. I really wanted to understand him; I even felt a little sorry for him. There was something there inside him which I had not seen before, not that I knew much of him, but I could see that he had been hurt and wounded in some way that could not be seen. I saw it for a moment and then it was gone. I took his medals with a feeling of hope for the future and guarded them with great pride.

Chapter 3

I am seven now and I don't go to school much anymore. I stay at home looking after my sister Laine. I feel a strong need to somehow hold the family together. I have become addicted to the harshness of my family life, and feel a sense of responsibility for their happiness and success. My mother goes out most days and I try to keep the house clean and tidy and feed Laine when she's hungry. I don't know where Marie is. I tried to understand my mother's behaviour; I don't really want to hate her so much, but I still feel that it's my job to keep watch on her for my stepdad when he is out at work getting money so that we can eat and keep the car running with petrol.

One day mum took us to town, a rare trip out, my two sisters and me, transported by a heavily laden pram. We had to go to the local government centre to collect some second-hand clothes. It was a long walk, my sisters were in the pram and I had to walk, as usual. When we got there they kept us waiting around, which didn't go too well with my mother. She had a strong, defiant sense of pride that was wild and unpredictable. People soon knew she was not one to be messed with. It didn't take much to set her off and she wasn't intimidated by anyone.

We received the clothes, put them in the pram and set off back home. On the way we passed through the town centre and visited a large store. As we walked through something caught my eye – a moving clockwork toy, a war tank, which was wound up with a key and then left to travel in the direction it was pointed. I was fascinated by its motion. There was something about it that drew me in. It was a sandy desert colour with black shades. There was a black cross with white edging. This identified it as a German tank, an enemy tank from the war that had finished just before I was born. This was the main attraction, a toy German tank for me to play with; maybe I could drop things on it and smash it. Trying to suppress my eagerness, I asked my mother if she would buy it for me, and to my surprise and delight she agreed. The tank came in a dramatic box with exploding pictures on both sides.

That was the first time I remember asking my mother for anything. It was a profound moment for me. She gave me what I wanted and was pleased to do so. There was a new understanding inside me that accepted her as my mother; we were both on the same side. Maybe I could ask her for things and maybe she would be happy to give them. All I had to do was ask. This must have been the first time that I had felt any real bond between us. I'd tried never to ask her for anything before.

Once back home I eagerly tried out my war toy, first on the flatness of the kitchen floor and then outside in the world of unknown challenges. What I did not know was that my tank was a reward for rescuing my sister from a man in a lorry outside our house the day before. The man had tried to snatch Marie from the pavement, but I spotted him and called out to the neighbour next door for help. The woman came out from her open door, grabbing hold of my sister just as the man was about to take her. The woman screamed and shouted at him and he quickly made off in his lorry. Marie was extremely lucky not to have been taken. I wondered what would have become of her. This was more evidence that the world was a hostile and dangerous place.

I tried to keep a watchful eye on Marie, but she was very self-willed and did her own thing. We never really spoke or played together. She didn't seem to like me very much and made a point of keeping away from me. I guess there wasn't really much I could do about her safety. She was left to run wild just as I was.

Now back to the serious business of war and mechanically wound-up tanks. I think I must have almost worn out the key that first day: backwards and forwards the tank went, crossing the factory road that ran between the houses under the archway and into the factory yard beyond our garden. I took my tank to bed with me that night, feeling safe and protected by it, even if it was a German enemy tank. It was mine and I had control of its power. I slept dreaming of war – what did I know of war!

Daylight came and I was up and ready to fight the battle for another day. A bowl of porridge and out I went, making sure I had the key to wind my tank into motion. I put obstacles in its way and watched intently as it climbed over all that I placed in its path. It was powerful and strong. Backwards and forwards across the factory road, just as it had done the day before; I was captivated by its seemingly unstoppable power. I sat there on the kerbstone watching, intrigued by its unknown limits. Vehicles regularly came in and out from the factory; I could hear one coming now. My tank was on the road in motion. I was being challenged by a force unknown to me, a force that I could only hear. I had no understanding of its capability, or of its power over my tank. Surely it would not dare to approach. The noise came closer and closer. I ran to the tank as fast as I could, I re-wound its power and set it off, back across the factory road as a direct challenge to the approaching unknown. I was sure my tank would stop the approaching force and survive the crossing; surely the vehicle would be forced to stop. But the vehicle kept on coming, crushing my tank under its wheels, and the driver never even stopped to look.

This was a profound moment for me. I knew there was something important to learn from it, but couldn't immediately find what I was searching for. But what I did understand was that my powerful toy tank made of metal and steel was flattened on the road, and I alone had witnessed it.

I pondered on it in silence for the rest of the day and all through that night until morning. I needed to have a second try at it. I wanted another chance, a new tank. I knew where they were, at the store named Woolworths with red doors, on the second glass shelf to the left of the main entrance. I would go there today and get one. Take it from the shelf and bring it back home. I must do it.

I got the bus into town and then walked to the shop, through the main doors and up to where the tanks were displayed. I stood there looking around; I had not been noticed. I could just reach up to the boxes. I took one from the shelf, shaking the box before walking away, out through the doors onto the street.

I had done it. The feeling was great. I felt so good I walked all the way home, going through the park on the way. I felt strong and content. I had completed my first mission. The feeling was liberating. I was in charge of my life. And I would now make my own decisions. I now understood that life consisted of a series of choices. This was the first time I had ever stolen anything and I liked the feeling – a mixture of excitement and fear, followed by a rush of elation, completion, success. But when I got home I found there was no key in the box, and the new tank meant little to me.

I now took to spending more time outside in the backyard and, after the men from the factory had locked up and gone home, I would be through the fence and into the factory grounds, which extended way back to a railway track with an old rail engine on it. This was to be my new place of learning, my secret hideaway known only to me. No people.

Summer was on its way, blue skies and warm sunlight to hope for, with carefree days that would guard me from thoughts of cold dark nights. Mum spends more time out of the house; I've given up on her, and now I am more responsible for looking after my sisters. Cleaning around the house was a normal routine that I chose to do, like my stepdad when he comes home from work. I call him Dad now. I think it makes him feel better and more accepted by me. I try to get Marie to help me, but with little effect. She's gone, out the door, disappearing just like I do. It seems that I am powerless over her. I am sure that life is just as difficult and complex for her as for me. There is a stubborn defiance about her, a solitude in her that I recognise from my own.

My mother would return home, showing little gratitude for my loyalty and efforts, but she had come to realise that I could be an asset to her. This gave me some power to use against her, though often with little effect. She did occasionally make an effort to show some gratitude and affection towards me in order to get my support. I quickly learnt to negotiate for money. Sometimes, when she was happy, she would sing. This would soften my resistance to her and her wild need to be free of us. She was clearly a passionate person. She would sing Mario Lanza songs with deep passion and feelings. Sometimes she would laugh at herself. She clearly enjoyed singing and, truth be told, I also enjoyed her singing. She was a different person when she sang. Her singing would break down my defences, and I remember once allowing her to put me on her knee whilst she sang about a little boy whose daddy had died and gone to heaven. In the song the little boy would ask, "Where has Daddy gone, Mummy?" and she would sing in reply "Your daddy has gone where the angels sing, my dear little one". I was deeply touched by her singing, which made me open and defenceless, causing a sense of panic and fear that I might sob and cry out from the deep pain inside me. This pain was so huge and scary that I was sure I would be lost in unbearable grief and sorrow, powerless to hide my desperate need to feel loved and be nurtured by the gentleness of a woman. If I were to sob and cry, my wounds would be open for all to see. If I let her cuddle me, I feared that I would cry uncontrollably. So I pushed her away with all my strength, not allowing her to hold me. I broke free of her grip and ran off into the garden, alone with my thoughts and solitude, and then to the factory yard where no one could see me.

How I needed to be loved, but somehow I had to protect myself from her and her sad song of a little boy with no daddy. I was that little boy. I had no daddy.

Summer was here now, which allowed the back door to be fully open, letting the sunlight shine in beyond the door into the normally dark kitchen. The radio was on with someone talking about the war and the terrible, evil things the Nazis did to Jewish women and children. The speaker spoke of doctors putting babies into freezing cold water and then into boiling hot water in order to research the effects, which resulted in flesh and skin dropping off their tiny bodies. I was standing on a chair at the time having my hair cut. The words coming from the radio were clear and well spoken, and I was drawn to the voice. I knew the Nazis were evil, but what I was hearing shocked and scared me, making me aware of the extent of humans' ability to be evil to each other. Standing on the chair, I felt vulnerable and exposed as if I sensed what was about to come. There was nowhere for me to go, nowhere for me to hide. I was trapped, open to all that was about to enter into my body. My mother shouted out "Fucking evil German bastards!" in just the same way she did when screaming out the same words in temper at Alfie. I didn't understand why she called him a German Nazi. Alfie had been in the British Navy, killing German sailors at sea.

Suddenly she burst into laughter and then started singing as if drunk. I knew she wasn't, I could clearly see she was in one of her jolly happy moods. She was extremely unpredictable; I never knew what she would do next. The radio spurted out more claims of cruelty by the German elite, the SS Gestapo, known to be the worst of all for their barbaric cruelty, the Nazi killing machine. This was to set her off again into a German military march, kicking out her legs at 45 degrees from the ground and raising her right arm up into the air. Repeating the movement she went from one side of the room and then back again, then bursting into laughter once more. I couldn't see anything funny in her actions.

She then spoke again, directly to me. The words that came from her mouth would change me, and my life, so dramatically that I would never fully recover.

"Your father was a German Nazi," she said, "SS Gestapo."

"Achtung! Achtung!" she shouted out, trying to sound like a German Nazi, and she did the Nazi salute again, raising her right arm up into the air.

I was devastated by her words. I went into some kind of shock, my whole body started to shake uncontrollably from inside. I didn't know what to do. I stood there motionless, unable to move. I knew I had to do something, but I couldn't move. I couldn't allow her to see how much I was trembling. I had to control the terrible feelings inside me, that's all I could think of. 'Stop the trembling, stop the trembling,' I said to myself, 'I am OK.' Surely it was a mad, sick joke of hers, surely she was not telling the truth, surely she was not talking about me.

I tried hard not to feel the traumatic emotions enter my body. It was not real. It was not happening to me. I must resist, stand strong and be untouched. I tried to block out the moment. Her words struck deep inside me, down deep into my soul. I was powerless. Panic took me over. Emotions were welling up inside me. I was traumatised, the feelings screamed out, but made no sound. My need for love called out from somewhere else deep inside me, wrenching at my body. The pain I felt was too much for me to hold. My thoughts had no comprehension. I was lost in a moment of insanity. The feeling now locked inside me, my inner thoughts spinning around and around inside my head, my heart sobbing and crying.

I hear from somewhere else, a place of unforgiveable sorrow and grief, the screams of children, the screams of hell, broken men frozen to the ground, and no women to hold their pain, their loss, as they die. Six thousand years I have felt your pain. Let me now fall down to the ground, smashed and shattered into a thousand pieces. Surely this day I will die, never needing to suffer this world's misery again. Oh the greatness of all pain, my life is yours. I am done. At your mercy, I am helpless in your presence. The madness and insanity of this world consumes me. Kill me now and spare me from the truth of those words. My body is crippled now and always broken. I cannot live here. This world is not for children. This day I surely die. Where is love and compassion? I call out for all that is just and all that considers love to be true. I call out for angels and all they may hold for me, in purpose that they may protect me from all that is unnecessary to my suffering in this life, for all I am, I am only a child and I will go as a child. I see too much of this world's suffering, the cruelty that is done in arrogance and vanity. I am locked in with my child; and the truth is locked away with my child. The truth of my pain locked into bones now, and no more a child I shall be, for this day is my last. This world is not for me and this woman is not of mine. Let me go. Spare me for I know nothing of these things and now I am gone.

I hear words from somewhere else, calling me back. My angel calls me to return.

'You must not let the foolishness and unhappiness of this woman destroy you,' she said, 'She cannot see you; she is trying to find you. You will survive this day.'

'What am I to do? I am confused. How can I ever let her come close to me again? How can I ever let her see me as I am? I feel myself falling into an empty void of nothingness. I see only rejection, detachment, and abandonment, humiliation and aloneness in this world of sadness. My child condemned into a lifetime of knowing only rejection and fear, with no compassion. In this world, but not of it – I do not belong here. This is a world of cruelty where people walk unloved and children are set upon, for they are weak and vulnerable, easy to use and abuse. I could never feel safe here. I would soon be found out, stripped and tortured, humiliated. Yes, this is me. This is where I stand, naked upon this chair, stripped of all that is of any value to me, tortured, humiliated, helpless, vulnerable, and innocent, a child of the universe.'

'What makes you think you are so special? Why do you think that you are any different? You are not the only one to suffer. Many have gone before you and many will *come after you. Have you already forgotten the truth in this? Do you no longer have a memory of where you came from? You know you are loved.'* My angel speaks on. *'You know that you are safe with no reason to fear. Yes, things in this world are painful and seem unjust, with cruelty and misunderstandings, but this is no concern of yours. You know that life is a wonderful gift, an adventure of the unknown magical possibility; take it in both hands and run with it. You will not be left abandoned. Embrace it, for you are safe in it.'*

Now my angel was gone, and my child was also gone, locked away in a secret, dark, cold dungeon somewhere inside me, locked in with a huge tormented monster of conflicting rage, pain and resentment. I told my child that I could find no other alternative but to abandon him if he were to survive. I told him to be brave and not to cry in fear of the monster. 'Show him love and compassion,' I told him, 'the monster will not hurt you. This monster makes terrible fearful noises because it is in unbearable pain. See if you can learn to understand and comfort it. Try also to love yourself, and above all you must stay alive and wait for me to return. One day I will come back for you.'

That night was very disturbing for me. Thoughts were spinning around in my head and I felt separated from my body, in my bed but trying to find a place somewhere else, outside of myself. I was devastated and traumatised. The child in me died that day. As I lay there trying to make sense of my nightmare thoughts, I couldn't help but wonder who else knew of my terrible secret. Did my stepdad know who I was? Did my eldest sister know? Maybe that's why she doesn't like me.

I was lost in horrific thoughts of not belonging, being different and alone, trying to survive in a hostile world, trying to suppress and hide my fear and terror. My only hope was Alfie, my step-dad, but he was always out at work and when he came home I never knew what to say to him. We didn't really talk much, and I never got any cuddles or kisses from him. I don't think he knew how to approach me; maybe he was just as unsure of my feeling towards him as I was of his. I recognised that he himself had not been loved as a child and I didn't see him get any love from my mother.

Chapter 4

I am eight years old and eldest sister Marie has little to do with me. We begin to fight like cat and dog, always taunting or disagreeing. She constantly complains to my mother that I have done this or that to her. This results in direct conflict with my mother and often some kind of physical act of aggression – she was always throwing things at me, which Marie seemed to get some kind of pleasure from.

My mother continued to give verbal abuse to Alfie on a nightly basis. 'You fucking German Nazi' she would call him. 'Eichmann' was to become his regular name when she was in a rage, giving out insults and abuse. Eichmann was a German Nazi SS officer, one of Hitler's elite responsible for killing thousands of Jewish men women and children. Eichmann had managed to escape from Germany after the war, and now he was being hunted down by the Jewish people so they could put him on trial for his evil murders. The Jews were searching for him all over the world. They were determined to find him and punish him for his evilness.

I didn't understanding why my mother called Alfie 'Eichmann' – maybe he was Eichmann, though I was sure that he wasn't – but now I had a new understanding as to why she sometimes called me 'the child from the sky'. I had discovered some facts about my father. According to my mother he was a German bomber pilot, shot down on a bombing raid over London, taken as a prisoner of war and released when the war was over, then meeting up with my mother, having sex together, resulting in my coming into the world. I am left laden with the emotional baggage of being the bastard abandoned child of an evil German bomber pilot, responsible for the deaths of British men, women and children, the same children I go to school with, the same children I want to be friends with – to me they are all the same! My mother is apparently a whore, having sex with different men, having sex with the enemy – a German prisoner of war. A violent woman who screams and shouts, can't cook, doesn't know how to love or look after children, calls me Lucifer.

I am very different from all the other children at school. I am isolated, though desperate to belong, needing to feel safe and loved. I live in constant fear, having no idea how to make friends, no idea how to play with other children, unable to talk, unable to learn, different from my sisters, with a feeling of not belonging to this family.

It seemed as though my mother now had a new boyfriend: she had dyed her hair a light blonde colour and wore dark glasses, hiding her eyes from the gaze of others. She was always out, which meant I would be left to look after my sisters, keeping me from school; she would often pay me money to do so. I soon learned how desperate she was, which gave me some leverage to negotiate terms and payment. I became addicted to the power this gave me over her, insisting on immediate cash for my services. As I became more resourceful and aware of my ability and assets, I began to blackmail her for larger amounts of money based on how desperate she was to conceal her activities and her visitors to the house. I would stand on a box outside the kitchen window, discussing my terms and conditions through the open window, but I had to be very alert for signs of aggression from her as the back door lay between the window and the safety of the back gate. Sometimes negotiations broke down and that often resulted in me getting a beating if she caught hold of me. But she knew and I knew that she had little choice but to agree to my terms and conditions if she was to get what she wanted.

I was quick to learn the value of money and the power it gave me over her. My assets proved to be more important to me than my mother was. This gave me a sense of worth, a sense of having some control. I desperately needed to feel in control of something in this terrible nightmare life. I needed to reinstate myself in some way, to be worth something, to have some power and control over my situation. My threats of passing information on to my stepdad did give me some control of her, and also gave me a sense of being.

More often I was to find myself home alone with Marie. We were left like wild animals running free and out of control. Some days she would bring a friend home. I began to like the girl and to feel a need to be close to her, and before long we were kissing, much to the horror and disapproval of my sister. On one occasion, with my sister out of the way somewhere, I persuaded Marion (I think her name was) to get into my mum and dad's bed with me. I wanted her to kiss me and have sex with me. I had no idea what was required, but I pushed up against her when we kissed. It felt really good and exciting.

Suddenly the bedroom door burst open and my stepdad Alfie rushed into the room in a rage. He pulled back the bed covers and struck me on the legs and backside three or four times. That was the first time he had ever shown any violence or aggression towards me. It was a shock for me to see him so angry with me, but I was really seeing something else: he had come home from work in the middle of the day looking for my mother. It was my mother he had expected to see in the bed, not me. That's where the jealous rage and fear was coming from. I could feel and sense the mad fear in him, the fear of finding my mother with a man. That is why he hit me: not because I was in bed with a girl, but because my mother was not at home, she was out with her new man. He knew it and so did I.

Alfie rushed off in search of my mother, and my sister appeared laughing and mocking me. I chased her out of the house and never saw her terrified friend Marion again.

Some days later the weather was hot and sunny and I was looking to get some money from my mother so I could go to the paddling pool at the park, the same park my grandmother had taken me to for walks before she died. Mum was in the kitchen and the backdoor was open. I opened the back gate in case I needed to make a quick getaway, then stepped up on to my box ready to negotiate.

"Mum I want some money."

"I haven't got any," she replied.

"I know you have, I want some. I want to go to the pool at Nan's park."

"I haven't got any."

"Just give me enough to get into the pool. If you don't give me the money I will tell Dad about your boyfriend being here."

"You fucking little bastard, you Judas, that's what you are! A fucking Judas!"

She was angry, but I still managed to get some money from her.

"Put the money on the windowsill," I insisted. She placed the money on the windowsill. Once before she had managed to grab my arm and it was all I could do to break free, but this time I was ready for her. I took the money and was off to the pool at Nan's park.

It took me about forty minutes to get there. The pool was packed with children and was very noisy. I had been there before earlier in the year. That time I had managed to squeeze through the fence, but today I paid for a ticket at the main entrance. It felt good not having to worry about getting caught. I had brought a towel and shorts with me in a plastic bag. I got myself changed and put my bag nearby where I could see it was safe. It was a very hot day and reminded me of my earlier days with my Nan, especially the last day we had shared together in the boating pool, slowly paddling our way together around the island, eating our sandwiches and drinking lemonade on the way. Days long past now, but I still miss her.

The pool was noisy with screams and shouts. Human voices all screaming at once, making a buzzing sound in my head. The sound put me into a dream-like bubble, detaching me from people and the outside world. I found the pool a little scary, but I took to the water anyway. The water was warm and I laid down in it with just my head sticking out. It wasn't quite deep enough to swim in, not that I could swim anyway, but I could lay there partly submerged, pretending to swim, going through the motions as the other kids did.

Suddenly I felt a strong feeling inside me, a kind of fear, but I had no idea why. There was something watching me, but I couldn't see it. There was danger moving up on me from somewhere, I could feel it. I looked around to see what it could possibly be, not really knowing what I was looking for. Then I spotted it, there on the other side of the crowded pool – four boys laughing and planning. They started moving out towards me, two from the left and two from the right, each one smiling and with a look of evil in his eyes. I felt the fear rising in me. I couldn't understand why they wanted to hurt me. I was struck with panic, overwhelmed and, as always, alone. The water was only eighteen inches deep but it was like being in the vastness of the sea surrounded by sharks, with no possible escape. That's how it felt – that's how it always felt! Once again my life was in danger and I was powerless to do anything about it. I fought the boys off with all the strength I could find, but they managed to force me under the water. I was gasping for air. I felt like crying with panic and fear, but that would not have served the situation.

Then I felt the presence of inner strength coming from somewhere; I could feel my angel was with me, in me. I was strong and safe. Nothing could hurt me now, and they were gone, out of sight. Gone just as quickly as they had come. I had no idea what they looked like; I can only remember their eyes and their smiles of joy. I dried myself off, put on my clothes and went home, trying to understand what had happened and work out what I would do next time.

I told no one of my ordeal at the pool. There was no one to tell. My angel was the only one that needed to know. She was totally aware of all my fears and difficulties. For the first time I felt that this power within me was more than myself. This was very comforting; it gave me a sense of faith and hope, knowing that I would always be safe from the cruel dangers of the world, no matter what came for me. I was not alone. I had to remind myself of this many times in the days and years to come.

Soon reality caught up with me again. The school board man was hunting me down. He wanted to know why I had not been attending school. The man that called at the house had a bicycle and he was called Mr Drinkwater; a strange man, I thought, and a strange name. He seemed to have some influence over my mother, which I found oddly reassuring. He insisted that I go back to school; if I didn't attend there was a possibility that I would be sent to an alternative place, which meant I would be taken away from home and put into care, away from my mother. I thought this might be an interesting option; unfortunately they gave us a second chance and I was allowed to remain at home. My mother was given a voucher for new school uniforms for Marie and me.

So off I went, back to school again. But this time it was a different school, the Junior School it was called, just behind the infants, a two-minute walk after I crossed the road. My first day there I felt more alone than ever before – cut off from the world outside, unable to hear, unable to talk, struck down with fear.

The new teacher was female, young and good-looking. Maybe she would understand me and help me. It wasn't long before I fell deeply in love with her. I desperately needed her to notice me, to like me, to love me.

I stole my mother's jewellery and took it to school for the teacher. I waited until all the other children had left the classroom. I went to her desk holding the stolen gift out to her. It was a glass broach with the word 'love' set in it, surrounded by flowers. She was clearly confused as to how to deal with my offer of love. She looked at it and then replied, "It's lovely but I am not sure if I can accept it. Are you sure your mother wants me to have it?"
"Yes, my mum told me to give it to you," I said awkwardly, almost blushing, with feelings of panic and embarrassment inside, which made me wish that I hadn't done it. I just needed to express my need for her to love me; I wasn't able to tell her any other way. She took it and I went home troubled by my feelings for her.

I had no idea what was being taught in the classroom. I would look around at the other children, searching for signs as to whether they understood or not, but I saw nothing to suggest that they hadn't understood what was being taught. I was stuck in a different world to them. I would gaze out through the window, up into the sky, looking into the clouds and far beyond, always somewhere else, always outside in my mind, always searching for something else, often thinking about things at home: my mother; my stepdad; screams and shouts;

my sisters; the defeated and broken German army; dead frozen men; millions of tortured and killed men, women and children; and the world, and me not belonging in it, not really being here, different, isolated, unable to learn, detached in my terrible world of loneliness and fear.

It feels like I am on a small boat in a terrible storm, totally alone, no contact with anyone, just me and the boat in the middle of nowhere, no land and no people. My only companion is my angel and she only appears when she chooses to. Sometimes the storm stops for a while and sharks come circling around the boat, waiting for me. But my boat is good and strong. My boat is my body – it's the place in which I live, sailing through this terrifying unpredictable sea of life.

Sometimes the clouds clear and I can see the cosmos and all the stars beyond, never-ending, unknowingness, and then I know that I am not alone. Then I know that I am loved and watched over. Then I see and know all things I need to know. I must keep going; I must never give up on my child. I must hold my boat and my mind together and just do that which needs to be done and nothing else. The storm will pass!

The children at school have now taken to calling me and my sister names. They make fun of our clothes and the house we live in, they taunt us on the way home. One day a gang of children surrounded my sister chanting names at her. For some reason I found myself rushing into the crowd, not really knowing what it was that I was rushing into. What did I intend to do? Rescue her, I suppose. I looked at her and she looked at me and then she took off. She was gone and I was left in her place, terrified, just as I had been at the pool some weeks before. The crowd seemed to grow to seven or eight, forming a closed circle around me. I retreated into my bubble, detached. It felt like going back into a memory of a previous life, the terror and fear of a wild crowd of people stoning me and tearing my body apart piece by piece, unable to defend myself, helpless and alone, no-one coming to rescue me, hated by the crowd. I could hear their screams and shouts from a place far away.

I began to feel sick as they closed in. I must do something to break free from them, but there was nowhere to run, nowhere to hide. I was fully exposed to them now. I had been seen, identified, found out; they knew who I was and where I came from. They saw that I was alone and vulnerable, different from them. I wore black plimsolls and they wore shoes. They were exhilarated by my powerlessness – they were many and I was one. I was vulnerable, but I had no other choice but to fight them off. Coming out of my bubble I started throwing punches, which seemed to take them by surprise. I felt strong in my mind and in my body, concealing my fear from them. I survived, and managed to get back home where I was able to lick my wounds alone in my cold, empty bedroom, my thoughts deep and searching, not finding any answers.

This was to be the first of many conflicts, which seemed to occur on a daily basis. Some days later a boy from next door came out of his house, walked up to me then punched me in the stomach, knocking the air out of me. The punch was so hard it forced me to double up and drop to my knees, unable to breath; it seemed ages before I could to get any air back into me. The pain was excruciating, I had not felt physical pain like that before. The boy just turned away and walked back into his house. I had never seen him or spoken to him before; I didn't understand why he had punched me.

It became normal for the kids at school to call me names and to chase me, wanting to harm me in some way. One day four boys chased me on the way back from school. I tried to outrun them and make it home, but they cut me off, forcing me into a road I hadn't been in before. I had no idea that the road was a dead-end, and I had no idea how I was going to escape them. I was close to shaking with fear. I ran into a garden and they followed. They started throwing stones at me. I threw stones back, but my single stone was no match for the four or five they returned. For a moment I stood outside myself, watching. I saw myself and felt proud to see courage, courage that was unseen by my predators. What could I do? I couldn't fight them all. My courage lay only in that my hopelessness would not be seen. I returned to my body and reassured that frightened child, letting him know that he was brave and loved, protected by his innocence. I felt his sadness, having to carry such a load with little understanding of why.

Then a voice calls out from the house.

"Clear off!" a woman shouts, "leave him alone."

The boys run off.

"Come on you, come on inside," she says, as if she had known me for many years. Go inside! What a relief, saved at the last moment. "Come on, come in and sit down."

The house was very big, clean and elegant, with expensive well-kept furniture and a piano to one side of the room.

"Here you are, love, have some cake," she said, putting a plate in front of me with cake on it. "Eat it up." She seemed very direct and very bossy.

"Where do you live?" she asked.

"Up the top," I replied, "by the school."

Just as I was about to take a piece of cake, she asked my name.

"Stephan," I answered.

"I'll take you home when you're ready, Stephan. Finish your cake first. Have a glass of lemonade."

Off she went, returning with a glass of lemonade. I felt safe with her and was full of gratitude. How I wished I could live here like this. This was normal. Now the boys at school know that I am not alone; I had a rich, powerful and caring friend.

She continued asking questions to which I made short replies – 'yes', 'no', 'don't know'. I always found questions difficult to answer, thinking more about the questions than the answers. How could I give an answer before fully understanding the meaning of the question? What was the true meaning of any question and what was the truth in the answer? All this processing took time and once I had thought it all through the need for an answer had passed, sealing my isolation even more.

The old lady reminded me of my grandmother. She would be about the same age.

"If those boys chase you again," she said, "you come and knock on my door. You can come here any time you want."

She took me back to my house. She knocked at the front door but there was no answer.

"We need to go to the back door," I said, which we did. I could feel that she was finding dealing with the situation a little difficult. My mother came to the door.

"Where have you been?" she asked aggressively. The lady tried to explain. She told my mother her name, Mrs Bunce, and gave directions to where she lived, about 200 yards from my house.

"Some bullies chased Stephan into my garden so I had to rescue him," she said jokingly. My mother showed little concern. "You come and see me after school tomorrow and I will have something for you," the old lady said to me, "Now go inside with your mum." And off she went without a thank you from my mother or me.

I did more thinking that night whilst in bed. I was a little scared of going to school the next day, but it felt good knowing that I had the old lady Mrs Bunce as my new friend to go to if I felt the need. I slept well knowing that someone cared about my safety.

Morning soon came and I didn't go to school that day. It had been so different at the infants' school. I had felt happy and safe there. I had felt loved. Now school was a hostile and scary place. I couldn't hear. I found it difficult to talk. I had no friends to play with. It seemed impossible for me to learn or remember anything. My mind was too busy with other things, such as fear and feeling alone and not belonging. I was in need of love and support, guidance, care and nurture, but I was not being seen. I wasn't noticed at school anymore. Nobody saw me, unlike at the infants' school. All the teachers noticed me there. They had loved me. It had been good to be there. Now it was gone.

The sun was up high in the sky now and soon I would be able to go back to the old lady's house to see what she had for me. I knew I should have been at school, but I didn't want to be seen. I was a little unsure about going to the old lady's house. I didn't want her to know that I hadn't been to school that day.

Anyway, I finally went to her house, just as soon as the children had left school to go home. I felt a little unsure why I was there and she also seemed unsure of herself, which made me feel doubtful of her intentions and motives. I wanted to know what she had for me but I wasn't able to ask.

"Come in Stephan," she said, "sit down at the table." It was a big, dark, old hardwood table, very shiny. Cake and lemonade were soon placed in front of me. For some reason I felt uncomfortable about the situation. She was trying to make me feel at ease.

"Did you go to school today?" she asked.

I nodded my head in an up and down motion, feeling sure that she already knew that I hadn't.

"Did you see those nasty boys?"

"No," I said.

She placed a writing book and pencil in front of me, which made me feel even more unsure.

The house was very quiet. I could see out through the double doors into the garden – French doors I believed they were called, I had no idea why. The garden looked just like my nan's garden, green grass in the middle and flowers all around the edges with a big tree at the bottom.

"Open your book up," she said, "put your name at the top". This I did – 'Stephan'. She then proceeded to give me a few instructions. It was clear to me that she wanted to see what I could do and not do, which proved to be a short task that resulted in me drawing rather than writing. I could not spell, but I could draw.

"You are very artistic, aren't you" she said. I made no reply.

Over the coming months I was to spend many days sat at her table. I couldn't help wondering why I was getting all this special treatment. Who was she? Why was she so concerned for me? I wondered what was to come of it for me. Surely it was OK for me to have some kind of a relationship with her, to receive all this care and special treatment. I decided to take it as it came, one day at a time. I had no idea what would come out of it or how long it would last.

In truth I was a little overwhelmed by my good fortune. I wondered if I deserved it or even wanted it. I decided it was OK, and yes maybe I did want it!

On leaving she gave me some money.

"I am going to help you save up your money," she informed me. I felt positively excited by her words.

My mother became troubled and jealous of my newfound guardian and friend. She tried to stop me going. "You're not to go there any more," she ordered. Marie also became jealous and nasty. All this made me even more determined to go. I was beginning to enjoy my privileged good fortune, and maybe I did deserve it. I made up my mind that I was going to take it and hold on to it for as long as I could. She was to become my new grandmother.

Rich, tranquil surroundings; a safe place; peace and tranquillity; the sound of a piano coming from the dining room, played by her very grey-haired husband, who didn't say much to me. I think he was a little puzzled as to why I was there – he wasn't the only one!

The situation became easier as the days passed. Soon it became acceptable for me to just turn up as if it was my second home. I enjoyed being there. I felt safe there. Life was easier there, no fear, just like my Nan's house, just like the infants' school, real love and caring, a regular daily structured routine.

"I've got a savings book for you," she told me. "Do you save your pocket money?" I shook my head and said 'no' quietly, thinking about the last time I had forced my mother to give me some money. How much had I insisted she paid me, and what had my mother meant when she said I was 'a stop above my station'?

"There you go, a stamp book from the post office," Mrs Bunce put the book on the table, "What you need to do, Stephan, is buy a stamp from the post office every time you have some money and then you stick your stamp in the book until it is full, and then, if you need it, you can exchange the book for cash. It's very simple and it's a very good way of saving your money," she explained. "You can see how many stamps you have at a glance. It will make you feel good and give you a sense of being independent and wealthy. You will be able to buy yourself things. You can keep your book here. It will be safe with me."

Hearing her words gave me a feeling of belonging to someone, someone who cared for me and wanted me to do well and be successful, someone who took an interest in my daily activities. It made me feel important and safe. I felt sure I could trust her word. She would not let me down. She was my new nan, just like my old one. She cared about me and was going to look after me to the best of her ability. This stamp book would be like a bond of trust between us. She would expect some kind of responsibility from me in our partnership and I would need to keep to my part in it. But I wasn't fully sure what my part was to be; it was her idea, I was just following on behind, trusting her to get it right. I knew very well that somehow I would need to make some kind of an effort to do the right thing. It worried me a little. I wasn't really sure if I could do it. I had not made any agreements with anyone before. It made me aware of something new – taking responsibility for my failings and achievements. It was a little scary, but I knew that being answerable to someone was a big part in growing up.

How lucky I was that those four boys had chased me into her garden! I felt warm and safe inside myself. I felt I now had permission to be a child again; it was OK to be vulnerable and get things wrong.

The next time I went to see Mrs Bunce she told me that she had spoken to the milkman and that he was looking for someone to help him on his milk round.

"How would you like to help with that job?" she asked.

"I don't know," I replied, as I always did when an immediate response was expected.

"Would you like to try it?"

I nodded my head.

"Yeah," I said, feeling really excited but not wanting to show it.

"OK then, I will speak to him again tomorrow and see when he wants you to start." It sounded like it had already been decided. "Will you be able to get up early in the mornings?"

"I'm always up early," I replied.

"Good, I knew you were the right one for the job," she said. "Right, let's take a walk up to the shops and see about buying a new stamp for your savings book".

Off we went to the post office. On the way we would need to pass my house.

"Is your mum at home?" she asked, "I will tell her about you helping the milkman next week". I felt embarrassed but told her I didn't know if my mother was at home. She went to the side gate with me.

"Hello, hello?" she shouted. I was hoping that my mother would not be in, but the back kitchen door opened and my mother was standing there.

"Oh, hello," she said with a smile and a little nervous laugh, which she only gave when she was unsure of herself.

"Stephan has been offered a job helping the milkman, but I first wanted to check with you that it's OK for him to do so. Will that be all right?" Mrs Bunce asked, making it as difficult as she could for my mum to say no.

"Stephan said he would like to help. Is that OK with you?" she asked again.

"Yeah, that's all right," my mum replied, trying to hide her resentment with a little smile and a second nervous giggle, not knowing how to respond.

"Will he be safe?" she asked – as if she cared!

"Oh, he'll be fine. If not, I'll give him a clip behind the ear," replied Mrs Bunce, giving me a stern look for the benefit of my mother. "I'm just taking him to the shops with me to get some shopping in. Is there anything I can get for you?"

"Would you mind getting me some cigarettes," my mother replied before heading back inside in search of money.

To my relief Mrs Bunce and I were left standing at the door. I didn't really want her to go inside. I felt ashamed. I didn't want her to see how bare and primitive our house was, fearing that it would weaken the bond we had.

My mum returned with some loose change, "Would you get me some Woodbines?"

"Take the money from your mum, Stephan," Mrs Bunce ordered in her commanding tone.

I could see how Mrs Bunce was working the situation to my advantage. She was an intelligent woman. We seemed to work well as a team. I did as she told me with a feeling of satisfaction of having control over my mother, who seemed uneasy and powerless in this situation. I could see she was also a little annoyed at being confronted in this way. Her authority was being challenged and she had been forced to conform to someone else's good intention for me, taking away her control over me – not that she really had any. I was a little surprised that she could be made to conform so easily when challenged. It gave me a strong sense of power and wellbeing, and felt like I was punishing her in some way for hurting me. Now she knew that I had a second person, my guardian and representative, caring for me. She would have to consider Mrs Bunce in the future when dealing with me on matters of conflict and violence. For now I was safe and on my way to the Post Office to buy savings stamps for my new official-looking savings book. I was excited and eager to see what the stamps looked like. I was sure they would look like money.

Mrs Bunce bought four stamps, and they looked very impressive when stuck on the page. The page was divided into eight squares, one square for one stamp. She did some writing on the back of one of the pages and then handed the book back to me. I felt very proud and important. I was now sure that I could trust this person. She intended to be there for me and give me the support and guidance that I needed if I was to survive my childhood intact.

Out of the Post Office and into the newsagent's shop where they sold cigarettes. I sensed Mrs Bunce felt a little uneasy asking for cigarettes. I couldn't help but wonder why, I knew she didn't smoke, but there was something else I didn't understand. But surely this was no concern of mine – I was now a wealthy child with a savings book to show off my importance, with a government stamp of authority to prove it.

Back home we went. We stopped outside my house. Mrs Bunce gave me the cigarettes to give to my mother. She also gave me some sweets in a bag to share with my sister.

"Take these and give me your savings book to look after. I will keep it safe for you. Come and see me after school tomorrow."

She came to the back gate and called out for my mum.

"Go on, in you go. Give your mum the cigarettes. Stephan's got your cigarettes," she called out to my mum as she came to the door.
"Oh, thank you. See you. Thank you."
I handed over the cigarettes and kept the sweets.

Mrs Bunce had told me to share them with my sisters. That night I shared out the sweets. We all sucked on our sweets, one after the other until they were all gone. My head was full of thoughts, concerns and confusions about my future, a mixture of fear and uncertainty, seeing many possibilities. My mother was screaming and shouting at my stepdad again, as normal, calling him a Nazi German bastard. How I hated the sound of her voice. I wanted Alfie to beat her and stop her screams. Sometimes I was sure that if she died, I would be happy.

Chapter 5

I am nine years old and I am not completely alone anymore. I have a secret friend now, a rich old lady, not far from here. She cares about me. She likes me and she is willing to spend some of her time with me and allow me into her home, giving me cakes and biscuits with lemonade. She teaches me reading and writing. She talks to me and tells me things. She is my special person and her home is my place of safety. I can go there anytime I feel the need to do so and she will be there for me. She will take me in. My mother will not dare to come there and I have not told her the house number.

I started my new job with the milkman. I got up very early each morning, but this was no problem for me, I was just glad to be out of the house doing something that made me feel good and special – and getting paid money for it. Some days I would get to take milk and biscuits home, which pleased my mother, but she was more interested in the amount of money I was earning. Then Marie started showing signs of jealousy, and I felt a little vulnerable in my new position of power and wealth.

It was only two or three mornings a week, but just what I needed. The milkman was a quiet man. He said little more than I did but we seemed to work well together. There was little need for communication. I could see that he was a sound man, aged about twenty-five or so. I liked him and felt safe under his guidance. I was sure that he regarded me as intelligent and a great asset to him, not causing him any concern or worry, easy to be with. Mrs B told me that he had said that I was a good lad and hard working, which gave me a sense of pride and wellbeing. Maybe life had some good things planned for me yet to come. Who knows what the future may bring!

The days come and go and I grow stronger. I never let the milkman down, always being there for him when he needs me. I continue to go to school and look out through the windows at the clouds passing over the treetops in the distance, thinking through things, over and over, trying to understand. After school I go to Mrs B's house for tea and cakes, as usual.

Before going home I would count my stamps to see how much I was worth. I was now buying two stamps each week. Mrs B would also buy a stamp for me at the end of each week. I even bought a moneybox for myself to keep at home for my spare cash. The box was designed as a treasure chest that came with a key. I hid the box in one place and the key in the side of my mattress. One day I came home from school to find the back door locked. I went to the front window and saw Marie stuffing her face with chocolates from a large box. I could also see my moneybox – wide open! She had found the box, forced it open, then gone out and bought a large box of chocolates with the money.

I screamed at her through the window to let me in, but she just laughed and tormented me, making faces of joy and delight. I couldn't believe that she could do that. I was enraged. I smashed the window with a brick and climbed in. She grabbed the box of chocolates and ran for it out through the back door. I chased her and caught her at the back of the factory yard. I punched and beat her down to the ground. She was a fighter and fought back, hitting me on the head with a milk bottle. She was wild like our mother. I was sure that she hated me. From that day on we would constantly find something to fight over. I looked at my moneybox for many days. I never used it again.

But she was my sister. I needed her to accept me. I wanted her to be my friend and to love me. I wanted to protect her. She was damaged too. I was sad for what happened, and we were to become even more distanced from each other. It was a great disappointment to me and made me feel even more alone in the world. It would be many years before we forgave each other.

I would go to Mrs B's house as much as I possibly could, she was like my new grandmother. I would always sneak away after school, running off to hers at the first chance. But the love and luxuries that Mrs B made available to me reinforced my fears and doubts. I was split; living two different lives, being two different children. Now I was able to see what I had lost when my grandmother died. I can see how scared I am of the world. How scared I am of being alone. I am scared of my thoughts and feelings. More than that, I am scared of being scared and, most of all, I am scared of being found out to be scared.

Christmas was almost here again and the school was doing a Christmas play, which I was sure I would have no part in, or at least that's what I thought. I had not planned on being in it, but somehow it happened one day and I got sucked in. I was terrified and immediately withdrew, unable to hear and unable to speak, paralysed with fear and detachment. But there was one lady teacher who insisted that I go on stage with the other children; there was no way that I could communicate my fear to her.

The teacher glared at me as she pushed me out onto the stage with the other children. I was sure that she hated me. She had no idea how I felt and what damage she was about to inflict on me; or maybe she did, I could see that she was a sick, cruel, angry woman and I had no idea why she was directing her torment at me. She probably had no idea either. It felt like I was walking out into a cage of hungry lions. There in front of me was a crowd of one or two hundred people – mums, dads, sisters, and brothers – in a big crowded room, sitting and standing, looking up at the stage. I looked back and fell into paralyzing shock, struck dumb and powerless to move.

I had been found out and trapped, captured for all to see, to witness my humiliation. My punishment was to be stripped naked and my body torn apart as I looked down at their smiling faces. I hear the cheers and laughter, I see only pleasure on their faces as they delight in my agonising pain and terror. I stand helpless and alone for all to see, my evilness fully exposed. I can offer no words in my defence. I have no defence. I see into their eyes, looking back at me. What were they looking for? What did they want of me? Am I to be their sacrificial lamb – the wicked child to be burnt in the fire? I hear that terrible sound of humans all talking at once, their evil pointless chatter getting louder and louder. I stand motionless, staring back at them with sheer terror in my heart and soul.

I stand naked, up high on a chair of shame for all to see, my hair falling to the floor. My mother marches up and down doing her evil German march, she laughs out with confusing madness and I see thousands of proud German soldiers being killed, torn apart in the misery of war: men and young boys crying out for their mothers; wives and children, sinking down, drowning in the mud. As many as there are, each one dying alone, far from home, their dreams of purity and oneness smashed and scattered like sand in the wind, having no significance. Only the memory of their murderous evilness is of any relevance. Tricked and deceived like so many before them, suffering and giving so much for so little. Thousands of women and children given up, all wasted, for nothing but stupid pride and arrogance. A dream of glory. Generations suffering in grief and sorrow, crying out with pleas for compassion, and no mercy before they are slaughtered by hardened Russian soldiers with bitter twisted hate in their hearts.

I come back into my body, still on the stage waiting for my end, and am pushed off the stage just as quickly as I was pushed on.

I returned home exhausted, in shock, saying nothing to anyone. I didn't feel able to go to Mrs B's house. I went to my bed trying to find my angel under the bed covers. I called her many times, but she didn't come. I sobbed, making a whimpering sound, calling out 'Mummy' again and again in silence, just like the dying soldiers did on the battlefield. Who am I calling for?

Surely I was calling for someone else, not my earthly mother.

I was concerned that my sister would hear me calling out in my sorrow and grief. I could not let her see me like this. I called out to the stars and the universe all night. I called out to God, to my angel. 'Please help me,' I begged.

The next day I went to see Mrs B. I now saw her as my second grandma, and was beginning to have feelings of love for her. She was my only friend and all that I had, apart from my angel who I sometimes couldn't find.

Mrs B told me that she was planning a Christmas party for the children from the local orphanage, young children without families, no mothers and no fathers.
"I want you to be here, and I want you to bring your eldest sister," she said.

Still depleted from the previous day's ordeal, I was very reluctant to make any agreement; it sounded like another problem to me. I wanted to accept no responsibility in it. I said nothing other than 'yeah' or 'hum', but I did tell my mum that Marie and I were invited to the Christmas party. Mrs B also called in person to request that we attend. All was agreed; we had been told to arrive between 3.00 and 3.30pm. We were cleaned up and dressed up especially for the party, and we set off together, not saying a word to each other. I could sense my sister felt uneasy, but she was just as durable as I was. We had no idea what to expect.

I looked at the children from the orphanage and studied them for a while, trying to work out what I could see. I realised that my sister and I were more damaged and dysfunctional than they were. The children from the orphanage were very clean and well kept, but I could not see into their minds and had no idea what had gone before in their lives. I could not sense how they felt inside, but I knew it must have been difficult for them without a family, no mum or dad to go back to.

There was Mrs B, with her husband playing the piano, her son and daughter fully grown, both being in business and very well educated. Her son had no hair – completely bald and without eyebrows. Both appeared to be in their thirties and unmarried. The daughter looked like Princess Margaret of the royal family.

There was a Christmas tree with lights, and under it boxes wrapped in Christmas paper of all different colours. One present for each child, a total of eight children including me and Marie. There were cakes, biscuits, jellies and Christmas crackers. We were encouraged to sing Christmas songs, but little sound came from any of us children. I was a little unsure at first after yesterday's experience, but all seemed to go well. All the children were a little withdrawn and shy. My sister and I were extremely hardened and thick-skinned. Well, my sister appeared to be; as for me, I was unseen. I tried to conceal my innermost feelings and emotions. I had learned how to smile when feeling threatened. People seemed to like me when I smiled. When I smiled it could mean that I was fearful or felt vulnerable, but I gave out signs that camouflaged my fears and insecurities.

The party was a good experience. I got to be with my sister for a while and see her vulnerability when around other children; it had not been so obvious to me before. I also got to see other damaged children, in need of love and guidance with no parents and no family. I returned home with my sister; our mother was waiting for us. I was confused about my emotions and what I'd experienced that day; I did not sleep well that night.

I called back to Mrs B's house the next day. The radio was on and my second grandma was listening to the speaker.

"Well," she said, "did you hear that, Stephan? They have discovered secret information in the Catholic Church in Rome. The Pope has been keeping secrets from us for many years – secret information from God about the true meaning of life. They are saying that the information cannot be released for many years yet. How can they do that? I will be dead soon, but you, Stephan, you will get to learn the secret and hear the truth they don't want us to know. You will be a grown-up man when the truth is known. There you go, Stephan, that's something to look forward to. That's very interesting, isn't it?"

"Hum," was all I managed to say.

"Do you believe in God," she asks.

I think a while.

"What do you believe in?" she asks.

"Don't know," I reply, still thinking. Those thoughts would stay in my mind for many years to come. Yes, I did want to know the secret about God, about life and humans, I thought, or maybe I already know the secret!

"What are these drawings that you do here – have you seen these things before?" she asked.

"I don't know," I replied.

"Drawings of devils and angels. Men in battle killing each other. Did you know they have these drawings and paintings in the churches? Do you go to church?"

"No," I replied.

"Does your mum go to church?"

"I don't know, I am not sure."

"How would you like to go to church?" she asked.

I made no reply.

"Maybe the seaside next summer," she said, quickly changing the idea from church. I don't know what to say to her. I've never been to the seaside before. "We can go on the coach to Brighton. Would you like that?"

"Yeah," I reply.

The day after tomorrow would be Christmas Eve. My sister and I waited for Santa again, but just as we did last year we fell into sleep and missed his visit – but he still left our presents! I was to get a two-wheel bike, not new but in good condition, and a bow with arrows that had rubber pads that stuck to the doors and walls.

Alfie took me to the park and soon taught me how to ride my bike. It was good to have a bike. It gave me more freedom, allowed me to be alone even more, avoiding other children if and when I chose. I was able to go places that I had not been before, switching quickly from place to place, elusive, out in the elements, in the trees, down to the shops to buy my stamps, and to the graveyard where all the dead people had gone with the secrets they hadn't told before they'd died.

Snow was coming. It was going to be a cold icy winter, but still I would be out of bed to meet the milkman. Christmas was a good time for the milkboy. I received money and sometimes even presents from the people in the houses. It was a little hard on the hands. Woollen gloves were not safe, they made the glass bottles slippery, so after a while I had to take them off. The milkman had special gloves with the fingertips cut off, so when I got home I cut the fingertips off my gloves too. This let me to work with the gloves on, keeping my hands from freezing.

Mum and Alfie seemed to argue most nights, always about money. It turned out that Alfie was a gambling man, always betting on the horses and that's why she would call into his place of work to collect his wages before he lost it all at the betting shop. But my understanding was that he mostly won! He was lucky, winning many times. We had a car now and we had a TV set. Alfie was constantly watching the horse racing when at home. He had a new job as a painter and decorator, full-time and good wages apparently, but it seemed to me that regardless of how much money he gave to my mother on a Friday, come Monday she would always be penniless. She was very good at spending money.

It wasn't long before she took an interest in my savings and the money that I received from the milkman. Many times she would borrow money from me; no matter how much money they had they could not hang onto it or save it. She even started borrowing from moneylenders and they would not get repaid, which resulted in visits from debt collectors and bailiffs, banging on the door. I didn't think there was much chance of me getting my money back.

The only time I received any money back was when Alfie had a win on the horses – or when I was able to blackmail my mother. This was never a good idea, as it would make her extremely angry and aggressive, always ending in a violent attack. Often I would need to fight off a beating from her and run off. Sometimes she would use a stair-rod or even the poker from the fire; more often she would use her high-heeled shoes. She was dangerous when she started throwing things. On one occasion I had to go to hospital with a damaged eye.

She soon left home with her new boyfriend. I think she must have been away for a week or two, which resulted in me being away from school again, looking after the house and my two sisters as best I could while Alfie was out at work. I soon became like my mother, carrying a stick. It made me feel in control; I tried to make my sisters clean up and tidy their smelly beds. I felt like a German Nazi with my stick – maybe I was evil.

Marie was always unruly, but Laine was always very obedient, with a sadness in her eyes for me, which made me feel some compassion towards her. I could see that she loved me. She was always looking at me as if she wanted to say something to me. She never did. I was unavailable to her emotions. My fear was that I wouldn't be able to deal with her sadness; I was too busy trying to contain my own feelings and emotions.

A few weeks later my mother came back home. I hated her, but I was glad for Alfie's sake that she had returned. I don't think she came back for our sakes. She was now pregnant again; I couldn't help feel sorry for Alfie, I could see he was hurt.

She was a hard woman. She would often say to me, 'I could have given you up. They wanted to take you away from me but I chose to keep you.' To which I would always reply, 'I wish you had given me up, life would have been better for me.'

She took to calling me names when we got into conflict. I now refused to give her any of my money. We were enemies, playing out a game of hate for each other. This became normal daily behaviour for us both, and was to last for many years. She sometimes called me Satan, or Lucifer, or Judas. Sometimes I would kick her cat or throw something at it. She would try to stop me going to visit Mrs B, but I would find a way to escape. I began to believe that I was evil, which made me feel even more detached and isolated. I was beginning to change and lose myself.

Some days Alfie took me to work with him. I was keen to help him; he was so fast and hard working. I could not believe what a determined, hard-working man he was, all to get money for my mother and food for me and my sisters and, of course, his biggest need – money to gamble on the horses, which I became fascinated with. I would often watch our new TV with him, willing his horse on to win. I loved it when he won. He would scream and shout with joy, and of course the money would satisfy my mother and pay for food.

I would often tell Alfie, 'One day, when I grow up, I am going to be a jockey.' The desire became stronger with age and I would imagine riding a beautiful, wonderful, powerful horse across the finishing line. I became almost as excited by the races as he was; but I could see there was a downside to his addiction: he lost as many times as he won, and unknown to me at the time he was a lucky exception to the game. I knew he was a very lucky gambler, but there is a saying 'the only winners are the bookies' and over the years I learned this to be true.

One day while at work with him, Alfie asked me to pick up and bring him a long piece of wood. I picked it up, turned towards him and heard a loud crash. The end of the wood had gone through the window and would be very expensive to replace. I was horrified, and felt I had failed Alfie. I could see that he was troubled by it; he would need to buy new glass and spend time replacing it. The workers were not sympathetic towards him; I sensed their disapproval. That was the last time I went to work with him as a child.

It was a hard winter. The pavements were frozen with ice. One evening whilst at the shops, I came face to face with one of the boys who had chased me in to Mrs B's road with his friends and called me names, but this time he was alone. I approached him. I looked straight into his eyes. I stood there, squarely, waiting for him to make the first move, which he did, pushing me back with his straight arms, high up into the centre of my chest, causing me to go back on to my heels, down and onto the ground. My body fell and the back of my head struck the ice hard, splitting my head. Picking myself up, I stumbled home, getting sick on the way. This meant another visit to the hospital and more time off school. I had concussion and needed stitches.

Soon after this I developed migraine headaches. I can't say if this was a direct result of the concussion, but it was extremely unpleasant to deal with. I consoled myself with the knowledge that one day I would have my revenge on that boy. For several years afterwards I was sickly and pale looking, and migraines were to become a regular part of life, giving me good reason to be absent from school, spending more time at my milkround job, getting in more money and more savings, more freedom and independence from the world. I didn't need to go to school – I was special and different.

I now had a new friend, Carl, from across the road. Carl's mother was Spanish and he was an only child with no father. Carl had a TV and a round shiny wooden table similar to Mrs B's, but much smaller. Sometimes I would go to his house for tea and cakes, sitting at the table, just as I did at Mrs B's, but now I was watching TV, a regular weekly series about two Mexican cowboys, Pancho and Cisco, with big round hats. They would always laugh. They were good guys always chasing after the bad guys.

I soon learned that Carl's father was killed in the war by Germans, which put me in an uncomfortable situation. Sitting at their table, eating their food, watching their television, I felt like a spy, a traitor. The house in which Carl and his mother lived was in a row of terraced houses with two houses missing in the middle, blown up in the war by a German bomb. No matter where I went I was constantly reminded that I was German. Carl lived one side of the hole and two brothers, Les and Alan, lived on the other side. I delivered milk to both these houses, which is how I became friendly with Carl.

I also formed a short relationship with Alan and his elder brother Les. Sometimes I would go to their house. I was always welcome, but it wasn't easy for me. Alan was the younger of the two brothers, one or two years older than me. His father had one leg: he had lost the other leg in the war. He never ever spoke to me. His sons instantly obeyed him as he snapped out quick short orders to them. He did not work, and when coming down the wooden stairs I could hear his creaking leather leg as he moved from step to step – clunk, clunk, clunk, squeak, squeak, squeak – and then he would appear. I could see pain in his stern face. I could also see he was extremely angry, no sound came from him.

"Do you have a mum?" I asked the brothers.

"No, she was killed by a German bomb in the house next door," came the reply. I almost choked, but quickly suppressed all emotions that might give away my true identity. It was never easy for me to go to their house, the shame and guilt I felt was too much for me to hide. I always felt scared of being found out, constantly on my guard, hiding my evil secret from them.

How I hated my shameful existence. But I still went to Carl's house for tea and cake, and of course, to watch TV. This was only once or twice each week; I didn't want to get too friendly with him. I would go there when not at Mrs B's house. Carl was a good boy, clean and smart, polite. Carl's mum didn't speak much. She just brought tea and cakes to the table, making the occasional comment to Carl with a Spanish accent.

My uncle Jack was fast becoming a role model to me. I looked up to him as a hero now. Often I would listen to my mum and Alfie telling stories of the past about my nan and my uncle Jack, when I was a small baby living in James Street with her. Unknown to me my mother would sometimes sleep at my nan's house in Jack's room. The story was that Jack had made a rope ladder which he would drop from the back bedroom window, allowing Alfie to climb up into the bedroom in order that he could get a good night's sleep before going to work the next day. Another story was that after we'd moved into our new house, Jack had spent a whole night stripping lead from the roof of a large stately home, and then wheeled it home in two wheelbarrow loads, two miles across open fields in the early hours of the morning, so that we would have money for Christmas.

There was also the time when my uncle Jack and his mate Charlie took me out one day in their big flash car. Charlie was a very tall man, always smartly dressed in a pinstriped suit, he looked like a film star with his thin moustache and tanned complexion. Charlie was a car dealer, selling big expensive cars, and that particular day when we were out he had stopped the traffic to let a funeral pass by. The driver of the car behind did not approve and started sounding the horn, at which point Charlie got out of his car. I watched in delight as he opened the bonnet of the car behind and quickly removed the sounding horn, throwing it to the ground, and then very calmly walked back to our car, driving off as if nothing had happened, carrying on the conversation with my uncle.

Some people were bold and special, like Charlie, and my uncle. They showed me it was OK to be different from other people. It was OK to have an opinion and be willing to enforce it. That gave me great warmth and courage – it was OK for me to be different! Charlie was a very enchanting and polite man, always easy to be with. I felt safe in his company. Alfie was also very fond of him, but I think Charlie liked my mother.

Winter had gone and now spring was here, which meant summer would soon follow. My milk round was still going strong and I was managing to save most of my hard-earned money. I had made a new friend, Danny. Danny was a strange boy, he seemed to be a little backward and he wasn't from England, but from Ireland. The other children did not want to play with him, which kind of bonded us a little. He was the son of a policeman, which I found a little unsettling. One day I persuaded him to take the day off school and go out into the unknown wilderness – the trees and fields of the National Trust nature park that backed onto our school. Unfortunately, we got lost five miles from home and there was a huge thunderstorm. We got soaking wet and were shivering with cold.

Because Danny had not returned home from school (in fact he had not gone to school) a massive search was launched by the local police force. I managed to find shops, houses and people again. I went to one of the shops and told two ladies that we had got lost. They wrapped us in blankets and gave us warm drinks, and then telephoned the police who sent a police car, which took us home. Apparently there was a great deal of fuss and panic caused by Danny's disappearance. No one had missed me, but Danny's dad and the police had been to my house and spoken with my mum. Danny's mum and dad were not happy with our friendship, and he wasn't allowed to associate with me after that. In fact I never saw him again. I think he had gone back to Ireland or moved away with his parents, as Danny's house was empty when I passed it. I missed him in a strange kind of way. I'd really wanted his mum and dad to like me.

My mum left home again for a few weeks and then she was back again. It was clear that she wanted to be with her other man. Alfie tried to give her what she demanded, but it made little difference. I began to think that it was my fault, and made more effort to help looking after my sisters and cleaning the house, even occasionally giving her some of my money again!

Alfie sometimes took her out for the evening while I minded the house. They told me to bolt the back door on the inside, and gave me strict orders that I was not to open up under any circumstances until they returned. I always kept my uncle's air rifle for protection. It made me feel safe. I was happy that they were going out together. I just somehow wanted all of us to be happy and normal, no arguments, no screaming and shouting, no name calling, but it just wasn't to be.

My uncle Jack was to get married and move away to start a new life with his new woman, who did not like my mother very much – but she liked me, which pleased me some. My uncle left his powerful air rifle behind which I was able to use now. I took to shooting at birds and cats in the garden; I saw no wrong in it, in fact I got great pleasure from it. I had lost interest in my Meccano set and didn't go to school again. The school board man, Mr Drinkwater, was still on my trail, always after me, but now I had an excuse, I was sick and under investigation at the local hospital. I was anaemic, they said, and suffering with migraines, and seeing some kind of specialist doctor, which proved to be a waste of time.

My teeth were bad and I had one or two removed, big ones at the back, and considerable repair work done. Too many sweets and cakes the dentist said! I was considered to be undernourished. That was no surprise to me; I survived on cakes, sugar and biscuits.

Summer was here again and I would be out all day on my bike going over the tracks that Danny and I had taken when we got lost. I was beginning to learn my way around new ground, five miles in each direction from home. This was a vast area in which I could be unseen and unknown – free and open to new possibilities. I had my bike and I had money for food and drink. I had my guardian and advisor Mrs B, and the safety and quiet solitude of her house when needed, and I still had my angel, always looking out for me. I would come and go as I pleased.

Days and weeks passed and a new baby sister arrived; her name was Reta. She was a pretty little thing, but as she grew up into a young child she took to rocking and banging her head against the headboard of her cot. She seemed to be troubled in some way, it was strange and disturbing to watch, and she was a very silent child. This meant more responsibility for me, more baby-sitting and changing shitty, smelly nappies. Marie would have none of this, so it was left to me. Laine was now old enough to share some of the burdens that our mother had no interest in or ability to deal with. Now there were four of us, from three different fathers.

Alfie was always working, busy making money for our wild mother and his gambling needs. Of course this guaranteed that he would constantly be employed. He loved work. There was no stopping him. And our mother, she loved money and more than that she loved to spend it on new clothes and fancy things for herself. She was a good dresser and a good-looking woman, just like a film star. Blonde hair and big dark sunglasses with an expensive topcoat, just like a hooker. She liked her coats, but us, we would have second-hand clothes from the WRVS.

But Alfie often had wins on the horses and then everyone was happy having a big spend-up until the money ran out. Then it was back to bread and jam and the normal screaming and shouting and name calling, and selling anything that was sellable, including herself. She would swear and call out to the neighbours "You fucking talking about me? You fucking cunts! I'll smash your fucking face in, I will give you something to talk about!" I guess in some kind of weird way I was proud of her fearlessness, that she was able to stand alone and not be intimidated by anyone, man or woman, no matter who or what they were. She was her own person and I think Marie and I took that on in many ways.

The truth of Alfie's story became clearer to me after listening to many stories over the years. He was not

Eichmann, the German Nazi half the world was looking for, guilty of war crimes against the Jews. His father was English, something to do with the British Government or the military. He was based in Germany just before the war and he had married a Jewish woman. Alfie's mother was a German Jew. He had one elder brother. Both Alfie and his brother were sent from Germany to England just before the outbreak of war. They were put in an orphanage in West London, never to see their parents again. There were several stories about the parents – one that they were both killed by the Germans –but no one really knows what happened to them. Alfie and his brother remained at the orphanage until they were deemed old enough to go out into the world. That's when Alfie joined the British Navy, at just seventeen, claiming to be eighteen.

Alfie's brother joined the Household Cavalry Life Guards, based in London, and reached the rank of sergeant major. On retirement he secured a position in the high-ranking law courts of London – the notorious Old Bailey, which turned out to be lucky for me. Alfie ended up with my mother after coming out of the Navy. And now he was a painter and decorator, hard working, capable of earning good money; and a gambler capable of winning lots of money and, of course, capable of losing a lot of money. His wife, my mother, seemed to be a prostitute and was always running off with different men, leaving her children to fend for themselves.

As for me, my real troubles have not yet begun. I am only nine years old and about to bring sorrow and grief into my life and the world. Sorrow and grief that would come many times, in many different forms for me.

My good friend Carl, with his clean, smart clothes and good polite manners, in the care of a broken, vulnerable and fearful mother, who had only one true fear, that she would fail and loose the only thing in the world that had any meaning or value to her, Carl her son. Carl was good, pure, innocent, and his mother too weak for this world.

"Stay with me a while, Carl, and see adventure. Be free in your spirit, trust me," I said. "I will show you the way. You are safe with me. We will climb to the treetops, searching out nests to rob of eggs. School can wait until tomorrow and the next day and the day after. You will not be missed."

"Come with me and climb up high, as high as you can go and still higher on to the tree tops," I commanded, "Up onto the next branch and again the next branch. Trust me, I know these things."

There was a crack in the quiet stillness of time in the moment between life and death. Just a silent crack. As if already done, he falls to the ground amongst the sharp rusty spikes, sticking up like flowers all around. He is still and silent; I am unmoved:

"Get up, you are not dead, you must go home first."

Carl has fallen to the ground. I go in search of a passing stranger.

"Come quickly," I say, "my friend Carl has fallen from the tree."

The man comes and takes him up in his arms and we walk to his home, not far from here. I knock upon the door. Carl's mother comes and I am gone, across the road home. Not for me, I am gone. I look back and see the passing of a bleeding and dying child.

Carl is dead. A lone child, whose mother's only purpose here was to give love and care, and now she also will be gone and done. Now their house is an empty house; once it was a home, a place of love. The big black limousine had come with flowers upon its roof. I saw it for myself. It was there, black and shiny, flowers of red and yellow, and I saw the brown box inside. I heard my mother talk of a mother's pain at the loss of her only son, and she was gone to the madhouse, a Spanish woman from across the road.

It was true; he really was dead – gone!

"It was not I," I said, "Not I!"
I have shame enough. No room I have for shame or guilt, no room left have I.
I am not the maker of these things, reluctantly still a child of learning I am.
The die is cast and the stone set. It is already written and done.

'Give me the child until seven years and I will show you the person in true.' I have understanding well enough.
Alone as a child, forgetting even now the truth and the magic of my lost childhood, lost with the arrogance of growing up in defiance of all things, claiming forsakenness and speaking of angels, without whom I would be nothing.

What of my grandmother's devotion to me and my many guardians, without whom I would surely be lost?

Who is next to fall?

"Not I," I say, "not I."
I am newly born and with angels that wipe my tears and shine lights upon my way.

I must not fail. I will not fail.

Chapter 6

I am ten years old. Tomorrow my family and I will move into our new home, a three-bedroom house with front and back gardens. This will be a new start and a new life for us – an end to the hardship and misery of the past few years. I will now have a place to call home. Mum and my stepdad can stay for as long as they are alive, but of course the rent needs to be paid every week. My mum and Alfie have a rent book to remind them, I saw it.

I am longing to go to the new school at the top of the road, but I am scared. I am terrified that my fear and that my need of love will be seen. I don't want anyone to see how vulnerable I am. I am scared of crying – I will not be seen crying!

But at least I won't be called 'smelly'. I did have fleas but Alfie killed them off. I don't have them anymore and no one need ever know. Now I will have a new house to go to, a secret place where the children won't be able to find me, a new school to go to. Yes, things are going to be different now and no one needs to know of my terrible secrets. I will be free to be a child just like all the other children.

I don't have any friends to play with any more. Carl is dead. His mother is in a madhouse now, I heard my mother say. Will she ever be well again? Why would she want to be? Carl died because of me. He was pure and untouched. Too pure for this world.

Mrs. B is dead too. When I first met her I had sensed that our time together would be short, that one day she would be gone just as my grandmother was gone. And now she was. One day when I visited Mrs B I had an uneasy feeling deep inside me that soon she would die. I began to shut down and detach from my feelings of need for her. I had to be able to survive on my own. This was to become my sole priority; in order to protect myself I must not become attached to anyone. The only person I needed to take care of was myself.

Sometimes I hear my angel crying. Why does she cry? I have heard her crying many times. I wish only that I could help her, but I am unable to see or reach into the realms where she dwells. I know this world is too painful for her. Angels can't stay here for long periods of time. If they do they become consumed and lost by the overwhelming pain and sorrow of human suffering. Angels only cry when they are on their own. Angels only die when they are alone. I want to cry for her, but I know that angels do what they have chosen to do and nothing else. They do not want us to cry for them.

My sister Marie tells me of her first memory of the new house. We were transported on a milk float to the location. Someone had written down the address for us. My sister assured me that we had ventured out alone, just the two of us, in search of the house, on a council estate that we had never been to, about three miles from the cold old falling-down place where we lived. The more she tells me the clearer the image becomes. Yes, I remember the milk float, how could I not remember such a day!

"Hop on," the milkman said, "It's on the way – just around the corner." The milk float was the same one that

I had been lucky enough to work on – the milk round that Mrs B got me. I won't be seeing her anymore. I wonder if she knows that we have got a new home now; she is somewhere safe I am sure.

It was a warm sunny day and in no time we were there.

"What number is it?" the milkman asked.

"Number two," we hastily reply.

"There you go, that's the one, there on the end," and sure enough there is a street sign fixed to the brickwork, James Street it said, and a brass number two at the centre of the door. Wow, it had its own front gate and hedgerows all around!

We looked in through the letterbox; it was empty and a fresh smell of cleanness came from inside. It had a front and back garden, and rows of gooseberry bushes, which we were quick to try out – a little sour, not ready yet.

Yes, this is the place we will now call home. This is our home. I felt good and excited and had a sense that things would be safe and abundant. I was sure that my sister felt the same way about the house. This was to be our new beginning; how could we not feel optimistic? Tomorrow is the day we are to move in and I can't wait for it to come.

Tomorrow arrives soon enough. We are all excited, and set off together in Alfie's new car. He parks up in front of the house, commenting that there are no other cars in the street – free of noise from passing traffic, he said. He brings out a key, a gold-coloured key. He carefully pushes the key into the lock and turns it to the right – this is called clockwise, he says, the same direction that the hands on a clock turn and move. I will remember that!

"There you go," he said, "A big three-bedroom house and it's all ours, it belongs to us. We are free to do as we will." What a wonderful feeling I had inside, everything was going to be OK now. This is the beginning of the rest of my life, and I'm keen to get on with it. All that has gone on before is irrelevant, it doesn't matter – it's gone, done and finished. And summer is coming. A new school to go to, a new house, this is our new home.

We soon settle in, we don't have much furniture. To start with I had to sleep in the same bed as two of my sisters who both wet the bed. It was horrible waking up in the mornings to the strong smell of pee. But soon I was to get my own bed and my very own bedroom; it was called the box room, because it was small and square like a box, Alfie said. I loved it. Alfie painted it for me; it was a good feeling to have my own room now, it made me feel sure of myself.

Now we have settled in I will soon need to go back to school – a new school at the end of the road. I have been down to look at it through the railings. It looks OK and there is a small park just outside. An appointment has been made for me to attend with my mother, an interview with the headteacher there. My mother is not looking forward to it, but we must go or she will be in trouble with Mr Drinkwater, the school board man; he's been chasing me for years now. Time for me to get into school and do some work on my reading, writing, arithmetic, and times tables (I believe they're called) – surely I am ready for it now.

The day soon came for me to attend the interview with my mother. It seemed a little difficult for her but she managed, and I was accepted into the school. I am to start at the beginning of term, in two weeks time. It was not necessary for me to wear a school uniform but my mother needed to get me some new clothes. I am now clean and smart, ready for school.

But when I get there I am faced with the same old problems: I can't hear; I can't understand what the teacher is saying; I can't learn; I don't know what to say to the other children; I have no idea how to make friends.

What am I to do? I am unable to tell anyone how it feels and I don't know what I can do to make it any easier, but I know I must find a way. The only answer I can think of is not turning up at school; it feels unbearable there and what is the point of suffering if I am unable to learn anything? How I dread playtimes! I try to hide, but there is nowhere for me to go, I just stand there hoping that no one will notice me, terrified that the other kids will see me and single me out, calling me names; terrified that they will see how terrified I am.

I lay awake at night thinking of school. How can I stop this fear and torture? I have no idea what the problem is, but I do know that I won't be able to deal with it for much longer.

I somehow make friends with another boy, he's not in the same class as me, he is older, and lives along the road from the school. His name is Roger. He seems very easy and happy and is very popular with the girls. He takes me home to his house to meet his family: he has four sisters and one other brother and his mum seems to like me. I feel safe in their house; I like going there after school.

I always go there after school now, they make me feel normal and accepted, safe, part of their family. It's a normal healthy family, warm and tidy, with an open fire which is lit in the evening, and the TV is on. It's so different from my house; I would like to stay there, but I must go home. I have my own family and younger sisters to be with, but somehow things are not right and we are slowly drifting back into the same old ways. Mum goes out most of the time, and she still screams and shouts; the house always seems to be bare and dirty, and meal times don't seem to exist, we have to take what we can get. Sunday is the weekly cooked meal, prepared by Alfie as usual.

It's not long before my mother receives a letter from the school, stating that they feel there may be a problem with me that needs to be looked at by a child psychologist.

I remember the appointment with the psychologist very well, though I don't remember who took me there. I sat alone at a big table and a horrible man sat at the other end. I didn't like him at all. I looked at him, and could see right inside. I sensed he had some kind of problem or attachment to his mother, which interfered with his recent marriage; he still wanted or needed his mother, or maybe it was her that needed him. He sat there in total silence and glared at me in what I could only describe and interpret as an aggressive, dominant and abusive way. I hated it. We both sat there in total silence for 20 or 30 minutes. Why did he not speak to me? What did he expect from me? I was glad to get out of there.

He recommended me for a special school for so-called backward kids with reading and writing problems, or communication problems. The Heath School it was called, a half hour walk from my house – it seemed miles away – I was due to attend the next term. Yet another new school, this will be my fourth school now.

My first day at the new special school for backward children: there were about twenty boys in the class, different ages, different sizes, different abilities, and different personalities. I looked around trying to read into their personalities and see their strengths and weaknesses. I also tried to understand what I was doing there and what it was I needed to learn. It seemed we had something in common, we all had a problem with reading and writing, and we all had communication difficulties.

Playtime is as bad as ever. I have no idea how to reduce the trauma of it. What am I to do? Just stand there, hope and wait for some other kid to speak to me and invite me into their world of fantasy and play time. It would be many years before I was able to learn the skills of playtime. For now there was no escaping the terrible feeling inside my mind and body. All I can do is wait for the sound of the whistle to end my nightmare, and then go back to the classroom where we sit in silence in a different kind of nightmare.

After school I can go back home to the safety of my new bedroom where I can be alone behind my bedroom door, which I had now found a way to lock from the inside, giving me total solitude from the outside world, though not the thoughts and sounds of it – the screams of my mother and my never-ending thoughts of the frozen German army lost somewhere in Siberia – and my secrets: the longing for my grandmother and the loss of Mrs B; my shame and guilt over the death of Carl, and his broken devastated mother. I wonder if she is still in an asylum or if she has managed to kill herself. Only my hunger and need of food bring me back from the secret world of my thoughts.

I don't go to school very much now and when I do I find myself in the company of a gang of two or three bullies. They had taken to me for some reason, this gave me a sense of belonging and a kind of safety, allowing me to witness and observe their acts of control over other kids even more vulnerable than I was, kids that always seemed to be on their own like me. But I was different from them; I was able to take care of myself if required.

In the gang of bullies there was one very dominant kid, different and more aggressive than the others. He seemed to control the others and instigated all the aggression when bullying the vulnerable kids. All the victim kids were clearly scared and powerless over the situation. This really surprised me: I could not understand why they were so scared and allowed themselves to be controlled in such a way and robbed of their possessions and belongings. I did not get physically involved, but did accept sweets robbed from the other kids.

One day I turned up at school in the middle of the 11+ examinations. I was sent along to a classroom and made to sit through an examination in total silence. I couldn't read the question so there was no way that I could attempt to give any kind of an answer. It was a very painful experience and I was constantly tempted to leave, but did not for fear of bringing attention to myself. I would not have gone to school that day if I had known.

Christmas was here again, time for me to get out and around the pubs singing Christmas carols and making some money. One night I went to a block of flats in a posh area and someone had left a present wrapped in Christmas paper at the front door. I took it and for the first time in my life felt like a real thief and knew that I had done something extremely wrong. This act of greed would haunt me for many years to come. I wanted so much to go back and find the people, and somehow explain to them why I had done it, but the truth is I had no idea why I had done it or why I did not return the gift at a later date. It was a copper metal tray, and had clearly been hand made by the giver.

Mum left home again for a couple of weeks. I felt so sorry for Alfie. I tried to look after my younger sister the best I could while he was out at work. Mum had run off with her boyfriend again; Alfie would sometimes go looking for her and I would go with him, running along at his side – he walked very quickly. I really wanted him to find my mother with her boyfriend, I was hoping that he would beat them up, but he never did find them.

I stopped going to school. The last time I went I got into a fight with a much older and bigger boy. I was so angry, I really wanted to hurt him, but I couldn't catch him – and he just laughed at me.

My relationship with my mother was becoming extremely violent and difficult. I hated her so much and wanted to punish her somehow. I still received vicious beatings from her; she would try to hurt me and make me cry, but she never did. She was always complaining about me to Alfie when he returned home from work: 'he's done this', 'he's done that', 'I am sick of him', 'I can't do anything with him.

"He needs a bloody good hiding," she would say.

One day Alfie returned home from work, I was upstairs in my room, and I could hear her complaining about me.

"He's upstairs," she screamed out, "Come down here, you fucking little bastard!"

Then Alfie called out, "Stephan come down here!" He was angry and I knew that I was in trouble now. What should I do? I could lock my door, but then they would know that I was in the room and would probably force the door if I didn't open it; alternatively, I could not reply, leave the door unlocked and hide myself under the bed. And that's just what I did.

Alfie stormed up the stairs and into my bedroom, enraged by my lack of response.

"Where are you?" he called out several times, and then to my mother, "Where is he? He's not here!" and then went into the other rooms.

"He's gone out," my mother told him, "Fucking little bastard!"

I stayed motionless under the bed listening for every word that was said. Alfie went out looking for me. Some while later he returned, and I heard him say to my mum, "His bike is still here."

"Have another look upstairs," she said.

This time he will find me. I must make a move – out through the window onto the ledge and down the drainpipe. I grabbed my bike and I was off for fear of a beating from Alfie. It wasn't so much that I feared a physical beating from him, it was the risk of breaking the bond of respect that we had that I feared losing more than anything else. But yes, I was also scared of a beating. He had only been physically angry with me twice before, and once he had thrown his dinner and plate at me, missing my head by inches, with the food ending up all over the wall and floor.

Now what? Where am I to go? The only place I could think of was my childhood playground, the graveyard, and Osterley Park behind the old school where I lived before, and where I had gone many times before to speak with the dead stone soldiers on the soldiers' war memorial. That's where I will go, I will be safe there. Off I go as fast as I can peddle. It will be dark soon, I need to find somewhere to sleep. I think back to times in summers past. Often I would make a camp out of the straw bales of hay stacked up in the fields – that's where I will sleep.

I remember well the darkness, the loneliness and the fear I carried with me that night. The stars in the sky, these are my elements for surviving life's traumas; they serve me well and make me strong and fill me with a strange knowing of somewhere else, the place where my angel comes from. I wondered where she was, I felt sure that she was nearby and would keep me safe. I slept well that night, warm and dry with a sadness that only I and my angel know. I had felt her presence watching over me all through the night, almost as if an embrace had formed around me, making me feel full of love.

The next day I went in search of food, the weather changed and began to rain. I had managed to steal a dozen apples from a tree and sat in an old shed that had a tin roof. Eating my apples and listening to the rain and to the thoughts in my mind, I felt sad and lonely, but somehow it also felt good, and just what I needed right then.

I returned to my camp of straw bales with the intention of spending one more night out and then returning home tomorrow; things would have changed by then and maybe they would have learned something from my absence.

I was up early the next morning ready to return home, but I had managed to buckle and puncture the front wheel of my bike. I tried to fix it and rode it as far as I could before dumping it in the bushes. My intention was to return for it sometime later. Walking home, I passed a police station. I sat across the road from it awhile, wondering if I should go in and ask for a lift home to reduce the possibility of getting a beating. As I sat there thinking and watching, a policeman turned up with a bicycle; he left it outside against the wall. I have no idea what came over me, I liked the look of the bike and I was sure that I could reach the pedals, so in a flash I was off down the road peddling as fast as I could, unable to sit on the saddle.

I abandoned the bike near home. Unknown to me, the police and everyone were out looking for me but, yes, I had made my point and indeed it appeared to have made some changes in their attitudes for a while. Alfie never visibly got angry with me again, and I was empowered and excited by the whole event.

Chapter 7

I am eleven years old now, and there's so much going on, the days and weeks seem to pass unnoticed. I am always looking for excitement with an element of danger in it. I've taken to walking along the outside of the bedroom windowsill, out one side and then back in the other side.

The police turned up one day banging on the front door; someone must have spotted me and called them. They asked if my parents were at home, I told the policeman that my mother was out shopping – I had no idea where she was.

"Have you been walking along the windowsill?" the police officer asked.

"No, I haven't."

"Is there anyone else here?" he asked.

"No, just me," I replied.

He came into the house and had a good look round, then turned and gave me a stern look, pointed his finger at me and said, "Stay on the inside of the windows in future. It's much safer, and you're far too young to die. I'll be back later to see your parents." And then he left. He never did come back, but the police did send a letter some days later.

I will be going to a new school again soon, that's five different schools in as many years. My friend Roger and I became blood brothers last week, both cutting our thumbs with a sharp knife and then binding them together, like we'd seen on TV in a film about American

Indians. Roger got a slap around the head from his mum – for being so stupid, she said.

And I had even got myself a girlfriend, Jennifer; she lived just across the road from Roger's house. But the relationship didn't last; it brought out a rage of violence from somewhere inside me that I hadn't seen before: she had wanted to finish with me, so I told her to fuck off, and chased her halfway home, kicking and punching her along the way. She started crying and became really scared.

Carol was next; I gave her a ring, probably one of my mothers. When we had an argument over something trivial, I demanded the ring back and smashed it up with a lump of concrete on the pavement outside her house. Her mother wouldn't allow her to talk to me after that outburst; I never saw either of them again. I knew then that something inside me wasn't quite right, but I thought it best not to think about it too much.

My mum has received a grant to buy me a new school uniform, long trousers, a cap, tie, and a school blazer, I'm a real schoolboy now with a badge to wear on my blazer. I find it reassuring; it's a good feeling – almost makes me feel proud, and normal like the other school children.

Alfie's always watching horse racing on the TV when he's not working. I am determined to become a horseracing jockey when I leave school, I want him to be proud of me.

I've started doing a paper round now, trying to save some money for Christmas. I get up early when the winter mornings are very cold; it's hard sometimes, but I am determined to save some money.

One day Alfie took me to the betting shop; he had £1,200 of someone else's money. I watched him lose every single pound of it and he never showed one emotion, not once! I was devastated for him, it was not his money, it was two weeks' takings, a tough scrap-metal dealer's money – the guy was away on holiday and would return in a few days time. But as luck would have it Alfie won every single penny back before the guy returned from holiday. I couldn't believe it – I was so relieved for him. How does he do that? It's just sheer magic and shows so much courage. What a brave man, I thought. His strength and determination gave me hope.

I felt safe around Alfie, believing that he would always find a solution, but money was a big problem, large amounts of money would come, and in a flash all the money would be gone. Mum was always buying things we couldn't afford and then during the week they would be sold for a fraction of what had been paid. And she was addicted to borrowing money from money lenders; debt collectors would always come banging at the door, and I was the one sent to tell them that she wasn't in, with strict instructions never ever to let anyone pass the door into the house.

Once I was sent to the door to tell a man there that she wasn't in. I opened the door and said, "She told me to tell you that she's not in, but she is in the kitchen."
I heard the kitchen door fly open. "You fucking little bastard!" she screamed out at me, and I saw a flash of silver coming through the air. A large pair of tailor's

scissors, huge they were, nine to ten inches long. They skim past my face and lodge in the front door.

"I will come back, son," the man said to me, leaving in a hurry.

I knew my mother was wild and a little crazy, but I was shocked by what she had done: it was an act of blind rage and extremely dangerous; the scissors were big and heavy, if they had struck me in the head or face they would have caused severe injuries or even killed me. She showed no concern. I felt unsafe, and more unsure of her than ever before.

I tried hard to settle in at my new school. I managed to get myself into a gang, the gang of four we called ourselves, all of us could barely read, write, or spell. We were in the bottom class of the school, the dunces' class, as it was known; the whole school knew that we were not very bright – we were thick and stupid.

There were about fifteen boys in the class. At first I was unsure where my place in the class was, I looked and studied all of them for a while. There seemed to be different types of kids in the class: there were the skinny weak boys; the fat spoilt ones – mummy's boys, I called them; and then there were the in-betweens who had no idea who they were and didn't actually want to be anyone; and the boys who kept themselves to themselves; a couple of fairground travellers – tough boys, they kept at a distance, not coming to school very much; and then there were the hardened, strong, dominant group of four or five. I had to decide where I was going to be; I chose to go with the hard boys.

I felt strangely safe now, I belonged to something, I knew who I was trying to be just for a moment. The gang of four – unruly and untouchable – Harry, Billy, Jacko, and myself. Two would end up self-made millionaires, one was labelled a violent criminal, locked up for five years and somehow working his way into the army and finally into the SAS, and the other one, known as a local villain, became the manager of a steel company; but for now we all needed to work our way through the last years of our short schooling. Some days that would mean getting our names on the attendance register and then sneaking out of school to catch the tube into central London for the afternoon, returning home in the evening. I would come back to a filthy, dirty house with little to eat, always needing to cook for my self – if I could find anything to eat, that is! I was ashamed to bring anyone into the house.

I was out at the local shops one day when I spotted the boy, Watson, who had pushed me over on the winter ice some years earlier when I lived at the old house in Heston Village. I had promised myself that one day I would have my revenge, and now was my chance. I approached him and looked him straight in the eyes, only this time I wasn't standing square on to him – I was ready for him. I could see the fear in his eyes and he turned and fled. I chased after him, knowing that he was mine to punish, I just had to catch him. He kept running, two hundred yards, four hundred yards, eight hundred yards. I called after him as we ran: 'I'm closing in on you', 'I'm getting nearer and nearer to you', 'Give up now', 'I'm going to catch you, don't be scared'. I kept imagining that I had a rope hooked onto him pulling him back towards me, slowing him down. "I'm closing on you," I repeatedly told him. It worked; he stopped, out of breath and weak. I was delighted – I felt like a predator that had hunted down and caught its prey. I quickly took him down to the ground and then began to bang his head on the pavement as I spoke to him, reminding him what this was in revenge for. He was powerless and full of fear, but I could not make him cry. That's what I really wanted, I wanted to send him away crying, but I think he was just too fearful and dazed to cry. Nonetheless I felt my pride had been restored, and I left him to stumble home alone just as I had done those years earlier. I was not a kid any more, and no one was going to push me around or beat me up ever again.

Some days later I was at home, not attending school as usual, when a woman by the name of Kate came to visit my mother. She was a bit posh, kind of middle-class and wore lots of gold and diamonds. For some reason she had taken her rings off, to show my mother I assume, and somehow one of the rings went missing. My mother tried to blame me for it. I was quick to see what was really going on and made it clear to her friend Kate that it was my mother that had more than likely stolen her ring. My mother went into a violent rage, taking one of the stair rods, holding on to me with one hand and trying to beat me with the rod as hard as she could, cursing and swearing as she went.

"You fucking Judas! You fucking little Nazi bastard!" she screamed at me, failing to make me submit. Her friend Kate tried hard to stop her. "Please don't hit him, Kath," she pleaded repeatedly, but with little effect. "It doesn't matter about the ring, it will turn up I am sure." And sure enough it did turn up: some days later I found it in my mother's purse. I would have given it back to Kate, but I had no idea where she lived.

I was into horse riding now, taking lessons and spending every penny I got on riding horses. It wasn't cheap, but I was very resourceful, always working at something and quite often I would steal money from my mother's purse if she left it unguarded. (My attempts to blackmail her were no longer successful.)

One day on the way home from school I got into a fight with two boys. They were bullying some kid from along the road. I stepped in, trying to be the hero, but I was knocked down and hit the side of my head on the kerbstone. Once again I had to stumble home, falling to the ground every few yards. I ended up in hospital for a couple of days; the blow caused damage to my inner ear, affecting my balance.

We may have been an odd family, but our neighbours weren't much better. I heard it said that the man next door would dress up in his mother's clothes. He had been traumatised by her death – he was the only child – and he lost all his body hair when she died. The family on the other side were Irish gypsies: the mother, a big fat woman, always brought big pots of thick cold stew into us, insisting that they were not able to eat any more and we must have it. It smelt terrible and always went down the toilet pan. In my mind's eye I could see what was going on in that house and somehow knew that the eldest brother, a big bloke, six foot something, was having sex with one of his sisters. She was about fourteen or fifteen years old. One day she slit her throat with a cut-throat razor; she survived, but they put her in a mental hospital.

There was also a midget girl just along the road, about fifteen or sixteen years old. She drove around in one of those funny-looking disabled buggies, a green colour it was, and apparently three or four of the local boys were having sex with her. It seemed to me that everyone was having sex with someone, and everyone else seemed to know about it.

Mum left home again and my sisters went into foster care this time. I never did ask them what it was like for them to be away from home. I went to stay with my Uncle Jack, now very much a symbol of what it was to be a man for me. Jack lived with his new wife Pauline on a residential caravan site out in the countryside by the River Thames – a different world: peace and quiet, guns, dogs, setting traps for rabbits and shooting down wild pigeons. I loved it. They both had to go out to work, which meant I got left to look after myself for the day until they returned home.

It didn't take me long to find Jack's shot gun and cartridges. It took a little longer to work out how to load it and how it worked, but I managed. I finally found the courage to fire off one cartridge and the gun almost jumped out of my hands! I quickly unloaded it and tried to put everything back as it was, believing that all would be OK.

Uncle Jack came home.

"I can smell cordite," he says, "the smell of a fired gun." I had no idea what cordite was or that a gun smelt after it had been fired.

"Have you had my gun out, Stephan?" he asked.

"No," I replied.

I was soon sent back home. I guess it was too much of a worry for them, leaving me alone while they were out at work all day, with a gun around, and me being so unpredictable.

Mum returns home again, she comes and goes as she likes. I feel sorry for Alfie – she's pregnant again. I hate her. I want so much to punish her in some way, I don't think there's much chance of that, but I will keep trying.

There's a film on at the local cinema. It's called Pinocchio, a Walt Disney cartoon, about a wooden puppet that wants to be a real boy just like all the other children in the village. I sneaked in the back door as I normally do without much problem, and sat on my own watching and listening. I came very close to tears – the wooden toy was just like me! I realised then how lonely and different I was, I just wanted to be a normal boy child, just like all the other kids at school, but I wasn't like them. No matter how hard I tried, I was different and I would always be different. I didn't know how to be any other way. All I could do was chase my dream of being a horse-racing jockey.

I spent more time riding horses than I did going to school. Horses were so very different to people: four legs, two big bright shiny eyes – deep pools of love. I saw no aggression in them, though some may well kick you or give you a nasty bite. I felt safe high up in the saddle, with an authority and power. And when I gallop fast into the wind I am filled with excitement, boldness and courage, feelings of freedom that remind me of a time long ago when I was a fearless warrior in battle. How I long to be free to wander the wide-open spaces unseen; just me and the horse, alone in the wilderness, silent and different as one, just like the cowboys on TV. If only there were horses at school I would attend more often and maybe I would be the brightest kid in the class.

The council estate was becoming a tough, rough, and violent place to live. One day a young man called Alan Jee was beaten up and robbed by a gang from the estate. He was left unconscious after a vicious kicking and died in hospital two days later. The four members of the gang lived on our estate, one opposite our house, and one just up the road. Norman Harris, who lived opposite, and Christopher Darby were in their early twenties, and Flossie Forsyth and Terrance Lutt were in their late teens. They were all charged with Alan Jee's murder at the Old Bailey. Harris and Forsyth were sentenced to hanging, while Darby and Lutt were both given long prison sentences (Lutt because he was only 17, so too young to be executed – unlike his friend Forsyth who was 18). Harris was twenty-three and one of the last people to be hung in the UK, and Forsyth was the last eighteen-year-old to be hung. They were both executed on the same morning, Harris in Pentonville Prison and Forsyth in Wandsworth Prison, one day before Remembrance Day, 1960.

I was thirteen years old and I remember that day very well. I remember Norman Harris, he was tall and slim built; his father died of cancer some weeks after his son was hung. Lutt's dad had caught me robbing his fruit and veg lorry one day. He gave me a hard whack around the head and told me not to come back, or next time it would be an iron bar.

Harris's mother will always remain a haunting memory. I watched her one night at the cinema foyer after the film, going from person to person with little response, rejected, broken, and very much alone. I watched her for five or ten minutes as she tried desperately to stop people, begging them to sign a mercy plea to stop the hanging of her son. I saw no signs of understanding or compassion as they rushed past, eager to get to the pub before closing time. She was small and frail, and was stumbling about, no words coming out that I could hear. I felt pity and sadness as I watched her desperate attempt to stop the hanging of the son she loved. She died soon after, after the hanging, just a few weeks after her husband had died of cancer. I felt the pain and fear of this world deep in my heart. I knew that I needed to toughen up if I was to survive.

At home one night I heard talk of robbing a garage, Mum and Alfie were desperate for money as usual. Christmas was weeks away and there were no signs of any large amounts of money coming in. Regular small amounts were of no use, they were in debt and big men in suits would come banging at the door. I listened intently to the details being discussed, trying to understand the facts of the situation. It was clear to me that they were desperate, which made them willing to take stupid risks. I could see that there was little chance of them succeeding, it would require nerve, extreme calm and quick actions – surprise and innocence was what was needed.

"Why don't you let me do it?" I blurted out from the corner of the room, "I can do it, it won't be any problem for me."

There was a moment of silence while the three of them gave it some thought, the third person being a friend of Alfie's from work who was going to drive the car. They were quick to accept my offer.

We set off in the car. It was a cold dark night, with not many people around. We agreed that I would go alone and take the money from the till.

"We will wait here in the car," they said, "Make sure you come back to the car this way."

"I will."

Off I went, positive, unafraid and sure that all would go well, as if already knowing that it was done. I knew that something watches over me and all I needed to do was trust it, which I did without a doubt.

I walked up to the garage and waited for a car to pull in for petrol. I didn't have to wait for long. A woman came out from the small kiosk where the till was. I stood in full view at the door with my hands in pockets looking cold and in need of warmth. The woman started to fill the car with petrol. She looked at me with compassion, "Go inside, my love, and get warm," she tells me, "I won't be long." She doesn't need to tell me twice, in I go behind the desk, I open the till, grab the money and head for the door. The door opens and she is standing there in the doorway. Oh fuck, I thought, but there is just enough space for me to slip through.

In a flash I am out and running down the road with the money in my pocket. Just one problem, I was running in the wrong direction as I had decided to lead my pursuers away from where the car was waiting. I intended to double back to the car, which I did, but I hadn't told Alfie my plan. I ran around the block back to where we had agreed for the car to wait. There was no car in sight; they had gone in search of me in the direction that I had run. I was concerned about being spotted, but the car soon returned, I got in and off we went heading for home.

Everyone was delighted and complimented me on doing a good job. I handed over the money – £35 in notes.

"Is that it, any more in your pockets?" they said, as if they doubted my good intentions. I had no desire for the money, I wanted them to have it. They gave me £5 and split the remaining £30 three ways. But then I felt a change in their mood: the amount was trivial, it would buy the driver petrol for his car and then last one or two days, buy some food and maybe Alfie could have a bet on the horses.

That night I lay awake thinking, unable to sleep, with a sense of pride, knowing that I had saved them from sure disaster. I kept going over the event in my mind. Why was it that I was so sure of myself? When walking towards the garage I had no fear, just knowing that all would turn good. I was bold and full of confidence. I thought about my angel, I somehow felt she was close to me, I wanted to talk with her. I was searching for answers but she didn't show herself, so I questioned my thoughts for understanding. Why did the woman at the garage look and sound so much like my angel? There was something about her voice that was so comforting and reassuring – maybe she was my angel! Why did she tell me to go inside? What would I have done if she had not told me to do so? I didn't have a plan, in fact I had no idea how I was going to get the money. I didn't even know where the till was, not really, I knew it was inside somewhere behind the desk top but I had no idea exactly where. I kept hearing the woman's voice and seeing her face and the colours of the headscarf she wore, which didn't seem to match with who she really was. It felt very dream-like. I was sure that I knew the woman from somewhere, she was a good- looking woman about thirty years old, and she was kind, soft, gentle and caring. 'Go inside' she had told me. I felt love coming from her. Why was she working in a garage late at night? If she hadn't had been there I would have failed. I wondered if she would need to pay the money back out of her wages. I felt a little guilty and sad for her, and a deep need inside me to say sorry to her. I said a prayer to my angel asking her to go to the woman and take care of her needs and let her know that I had meant her no harm and thank her for the love she showed.

The incident was soon forgotten and no one ever spoke of it again, but I was sure that my mum and Alfie felt shameful for allowing me to do it. But I was proud, for me it was a sure indication that I was growing up and capable of looking after myself. I was not a child anymore. I was a teenager and capable of making decisions, which I had been doing for years anyway. I felt that I needed no one, and when things got dangerous and tough my angel was there, always taking care of me when I really needed her. I was safe and loved from somewhere else, but I wasn't really sure who I was, or what I was supposed to be, or become.

A new family moved into the street, next door to the Harris's house, a husband and wife and two sons. I became good friends with the younger boy, J-Mac his name was. He was the same age as me and he started attending the same school as me, but in a different class – he wasn't seen to be dim enough to be placed in my class. He was a military fanatic and his older brother was in the Queen's Guards. There was military kit and equipment all around the house, old guns and a bolt-action 22 rifle, which he had fitted with a new firing pin, re-arming it. We would often shoot out of his bedroom window at targets at the bottom of the garden; I was able to hit a threepenny bit at 25 yards. Once we cut up a bike frame and used it like a mortar, filling it with gunpowder and firing ballbearings and pebbles out of the tube up into the air. One day a large pebble went up and then back down under the force of gravity, going straight through the roof next door. We didn't use it again after that. J-Mac joined the local army cadet force, and sometime later persuaded me to go along and join. I wouldn't have done it without his encouragement. I was shy, timid and felt inferior because I couldn't read and write.

But I went along and it was great fun. There was an indoor shooting range, 22 calibre rounds, the same as the one J-Mac had at home, so on occasion some rounds would go missing. Summer camp was great, using and firing all kinds of weapons and guns, including the Bren gun, 303 bolt-action riffles, SMG 9mm sub-machine guns and sometimes riding around on the top of tanks – very dusty!

We would all sleep in billets – huts with ten beds on each side and a coke-burning cast-iron stove at the centre. There was a lot of screaming and shouting from senior boys, cleaning of kit, and in the mornings we would have to make our bedding up into neat square folded boxes: blanket, sheet, blanket, sheet, blanket. Then we and the room kit would get inspected – not really my kind of thing at the time, but I had no idea how important it was going to be for me later. It all was to serve me really well, but my time there was to be short.

Back at the unit there was a girl that came on training nights serving in the so-called NAAFI shop, which was opened up after training, for tea, coffee, cakes, and so on. I soon found out that after shutdown the girl would make herself available to the lads, four or five of them, behind one of the training blocks, a narrow space between the building and the outer brick wall. One or two nights I joined in the fun. The word soon got around, and it wasn't long before the commanding officer got to hear about the activities. He set a trap for us, but we all managed to get away in different directions – I went over the wall. The girl was captured and questioned, and the only name that she was willing to admit to was mine. I hardly knew her, I had only been there a couple of times, but I was the one that was kicked out! I was really gutted and it depleted my new found confidence. I wanted to confront her about naming me, but I felt it best to stay away, so I was soon back to my horses and my desires and dreams of becoming a racing jockey.

Chapter 8

I am fourteen. No more beatings from my mother, I am grown up now. I've got four younger sisters to look after, which makes me feel a little uneasy. Alfie is working hard every day, trying to pay off all the debt collectors; there's just never enough money to go round, he's over at the betting office now, trying to win some money.

Mum has still got her boyfriend and it seems Alfie has met him. He's got a wife and three children, two boys and a girl, and now everyone seems to be friends. We have been invited over to their house to meet the family. I am not too keen on the idea myself, but I agree to go along just to see what's really going on. It's all too friendly; everyone seems to get long, but I can't make much sense of it, I find it a little sick and strange. There is something not right, something about it that I just can't see. I am sure Alfie's only doing what he thinks is best.

Some months into the friendship and several visits later, my sister Marie and I have a trip out with the eldest of the sons, Cyril is his name, he is 13 years old, and there's something a little strange about him. He invites us to go on an adventure to the nearby gravel pits. We were quick to take up his offer. The gravel pits were a little scary – large areas full of water and no people around, eerie and quiet, large craters, holes in the ground, bomb holes made by German bombs dropped in the war, the war I was still trying to forget.

There were many deep bomb holes and a lot of them are full of stinging nettles. I have no idea why, or what it was that seemed to enter into our minds, Marie and I just looked at each other and, without a word, we smiled with excitement and pushed Cyril off the edge and down into one of the pits full of stinging nettles. We ran off laughing, and the more he screamed the more we laughed with exhilaration. We ran most of the way home, and claimed that it was an accident. He was to die of cancer some six months later.

My mother still carried on seeing the father and his wife, I am sure the three of them were having sex together. Alfie just accepted things as they were, but me, I hated them and wanted to harm them in some way.

One day Alfie didn't come home and we were told he was in prison for non-payment of debts. I was devastated. Even my mum was shocked and concerned for him; without him she was completely useless, and more to the point she was penniless, but as always her answer was to borrow money from somewhere or someone.

Alfie was only in for a few days – Mum managed to pay off the bailiffs and debtors. I began to look at her in a different light, she wasn't all bad, in fact she was a big-hearted person and very different from other mums. But I couldn't stop myself hating her. Sometimes she would try to show me some love and caring, but I quickly rejected it; there was no way I was going to open myself up to her, I was just too vulnerable I guess! I needed to protect myself from her the best way I could and that meant shutting down any loving feelings towards her. She was hard and tough and I had never seen her cry, though once she almost cried when I shot her in the arm with my pellet gun. But sometimes it was clear to me that she was a spiritual kind of person, and she had moments when she was caring, compassionate and kind, I had seen it many times. She liked to have fun and laugh, she had a sense of passion and romance, I just could not quite understand her ways. I remember her telling me 'one day you will understand'.

Alfie was glad to be home, he didn't like it in prison, he needed his cigarettes too much. The thing I saw most was that in a strange way there was a sense of him feeling safe and belonging with my mother, he had a purpose. She rescued him when he needed her most. I saw something missing in his life: losing his father and mother to the Germans and being placed in an orphanage must have made him feel abandoned. He didn't see his brother much. He rarely came to visit him; it seemed his wife wasn't too keen on my mum, so they kept away. I think the real main reason was my mother was always trying to borrow money from them and there would be little or no chance of them ever getting it back.

I saw a small change in the relationship between Alfie and my mother; it warmed me and gave me some hope, but I was slowly becoming hardened against feelings of caring about any one else.

I couldn't wait to leave school; I always seemed to be in trouble, with regular visits to the headmaster for a caning. If I wasn't getting punished by the headmaster it would be the deputy master – he was even more vicious, sometimes my hands would hurt for days. It didn't make any sense to me to damage my hands and then expect me to be able to sit and write afterwards. I always took a few days off school in response to their aggression. Some of the other teachers would use a rubber slipper on your backside whilst you were ordered to touch your toes. Rulers were a preferred weapon of punishment – right across the knuckles! There was one woman teacher that was always hitting me on the head with a big hard book, or she would slap me across the side of my head, this would make my ears ring. I don't think she liked me very much, but I had no idea what it was that I had done wrong, I didn't talk very much, not like the other children, they were always noisy, maybe I just spoke at the wrong times. I sometimes felt like hitting her back, she was a horrible bitch; it was a good thing I didn't get to see her too often.

As a gang, the four of us took pride in vandalising the classroom at playtime – well I did! We would break into the classrooms and smash them up, making them unusable. I loved it, pay back for the pain inflicted on us. One winter I took a hacksaw into school and selected heating pipes and radiators to cut through. This was very effective; they closed the school down and sent us home for a couple of days. I loved the sense of power it gave me, the feeling of rebellious retribution in my soul – at last I was someone to take notice of.

Me and Jacko were becoming very close friends now, we were both very defiant. Harry and Billy were more sensible, but influenced by Jacko and myself. One day the four of us broke into the drama room and went about smashing things up. The teacher, Mr Edmonds, came in earlier than we had expected and we all dashed under the stage. "OK Golf, come out! And the other one, I've seen you both," he said. Golf was Harry's surname and he was quick to move out, but that left three of us. Jacko kicked Billy indicating for him to go; he refused at first, but then I join in, thinking that he would put all of us at risk of being discovered. So Billy went out with Harry, and they received three strokes of the cane from the headmaster; Jacko and I escaped unseen.

Jacko and I took to working on a local farm very near to where I lived before, that old rundown cottage in Heston Village opposite the infants school, the one I had longed to go to all those years earlier, and received cuddles and love. That seemed a different lifetime. Now I was going to work and getting paid good money. The farm was owned by three brothers: the eldest was Charlie, the boss man; he didn't say much but I knew that he respected and valued me and Jacko; we always worked hard and as many hours as we possibly could. Every two weeks he would take us to Covent Garden, the fruit and veg market in the centre of London; we would get there at 3am in the morning.

We loved it, all the men carrying baskets full of fruit and vegetables on the top of their heads, some of them three, four or even five boxes. The noise and the hustle and bustle of deals being made called out into the early morning, money changing hands, but what I liked most was that I felt that I was valued, and even liked, and we were paid real wages.

Me and Jacko became a good working team, always there for each other. We only had one bike between us, but we would go two up on it. We went everywhere together. I started going to his house and got friendly with his dad. His dad was a real tough man, a big ex-army boxing champion, an ex-docker from the East End of London, a fighter and a drinker.

Jacko had two other brothers, one older and one younger, and a younger sister. His mother was tiny and very kind, but there was a hardness that came with her, like many women that had lived through the war. I liked her, in fact I liked all the family and wished I was part of it.

The situation at school was hopeless, and one day I took a horse from the stables into the school playground just to show my defiance of their rules and control over me. It did cause a stir! A crowd of kids gathered around the horse and one of the teachers came over and said I would need to leave the playground – which I did.

Me and Jacko took to shoplifting at lunch break and would return to school with gifts for the girls in the girls' school next door, which made us very popular. Jacko was always bold, even bolder than me.

I had been in touch with a horseracing trainer and got a promise to start employment as an apprentice jockey when I was able to leave school, as long as I was the right weight. At fourteen years old I weighed seven stone. I spent the next nine months starving myself. I only put on seven pounds, which I thought was an achievement for a growing lad, but when the time came I got a letter from the stables saying I was too heavy and they felt I was not suitable for a jockey.

I was shattered; my heart was set on being a jockey and making Alfie proud of me. I couldn't think of becoming anything else. What was I going to do now?

There was no point going to school anymore so I left before the end of the school year, and was barely able to read or spell. Now I was becoming wild and uncontrollable, devastated by my failing to become a jockey. I took to riding motorbikes around the streets and gravel pits.

Jacko wasn't really into motorbikes he preferred to chase after girls; I would often go with him to meet up with girls at their homes while their parents were out at work and the girls away from school. Often these girls were running around the house dressed only in their knickers. It seemed to me that they were more interested in having sex with each other than with boys; I opened a bedroom door to find three girls in bed together. Jacko was having regular sex with one of the girls, but she was also having sex with the local butch lesbian, who was extremely aggressive about the situation. Jacko had to fight her on two occasions that I knew of: she was much taller and bigger than him, and I think he found it hard to fight her off.

While out in central London one night with Jacko, I bought three Purple Heart pills. This was the first time that I had ever tried drugs. Just minutes after buying the tablets I was pounced on by three young plain-clothes police officers, arrested, and put before a juvenile court the next day. They remanded me in custody for two weeks in a secure institution for juveniles, asking for reports on me. This was a bit of a shock to me: until then I had never been answerable to anyone really, I had always done what I wanted to do, always free to come and go as I wanted, when I wanted – free to roam. Nobody told me what to do.

That two weeks seemed to take forever, I got a new understanding of life – it occurred to me that I had no idea what really went on outside of my own world. I was allocated to a dormitory with beds down opposite sides of the room, very similar to army billets, the difference being that the building was large and solid, built of bricks, while the army ones were made of wood. The bedding needed to be folded up each day, but unlike in army cadets there was no bullshit inspection, looking for dirt and shouting at people, everyone seemed to know what was required and just quietly got on and did it. I was surprised.

The food was good; we all sat at tables in the dining hall, and there didn't seem to be too much fear or aggression. I couldn't understand why it seemed to flow along so easily. There was an indoor swimming pool to be used at weekends, and a daily routine of simple exercise, squats, press ups, sit ups, etc., followed by a game of murder ball. This was extremely rough and very demanding physically, consisting of two teams made up of equal number of boys of a similar range of ability and size. The aim was to get the big heavy leather ball, which was three times the size of a football, behind the apposing team by any means – maybe this is why it was called murder ball! I found the game empowering, I was good at it: it required strength, aggression, stamina and lots of determination. I seem to have all the requirements. The staff, all men, kept a low profile, but I did pick up on one or two negative vibes; I was sure that unseen and unknown acts of a sexual nature went on at night. In the dormitory there seemed to be a high level of sexual activity going on after lights out, I can't say that I really wanted to know, but I did see boys getting into beds with other boys after dark.

My only interest and concern was getting out and back home, I had no idea what they intended to do with me. There seemed to be concern about my lack of schooling and inability to read and write at the level expected. I was there to be assessed on my IQ level, my ability to function and take care of myself, and my ability to interact with others. They sent me along to see some boffin guy in an office at the end of the corridor. He asked me questions and wrote my replies down on a sheet of paper, then he gave me little tasks to complete and sat there with a stopwatch timing me. Unbeknown to me he was assessing my ability to solve problems, and estimating my level of intelligence, IQ. I later found out that I had impressed him; he had assessed me as being highly intelligent and well above average IQ. I was soon released and sent back home with a pat on the back and handshakes all round. I had told the court that I had a job to start when they released me. The court was impressed with the reports and allowed me to go back home.

I was fifteen years old and ready for my first grown up and official job. I started work at a fruit and veg stall in the main high street. My previous job meant I had the skills I needed for this. I found I could easily lift up and carry a sixty-pound box of oranges on my shoulder, supported by one arm, and the people at the market were amazed by my strength! I had learnt how to do it by studying the barrow boys in Covent Garden. The other thing that made me suitable for the job was that I was extremely good with money.

I was quickly accepted and they liked me; I was also a favourite with the ladies, they would always ask after me and comment on what a nice, polite and good-looking boy I was. My governor, Mr Billings, was also very good to me, he was always saying that one day he and one of the girls from the office were going to adopt me.

Things were looking good and I settled in and enjoyed the job very much. I had to learn to call out the prices of cauliflowers, bananas, cabbages, tomatoes, fresh fruit and veg – 'Cheap here today!' I was a little shy at first, but I soon got the hang of it. It boosted my confidence and popularity, but things were to change.

After a few weeks I had a little run in with one of the butchers there; he got stroppy and verbal with me, so I punched him in the head and knocked him out cold. Nothing was said or reported, but things were not quite the same again.

It was not long before Mum and Alfie showed some interest in my control of money going in the till. One day they made a suggestion about robbing the till; I said I would think about it. I worked out a little plan, very simple, where I could get them £200. I didn't think it would be a big drama, Christmas was coming and as always they were desperate for money, and I agreed to set it up.

I don't know why I agreed, I didn't really want to do it, my loyalty was to my governor and to my job and of course myself, but I also felt a responsibility to my family – if I could get them some money for Christmas I would. In a strange kind of way I felt it was the right and noble thing to do.

I took in as many large notes as possible and bagged up £200 in one of the brown paper bags used to put fruit and veg into. Alfie came up asking for bananas, I took a ten-pound note from him and handed over the bag containing the £200. He walked off, I left the till open and went in search of change for the ten pound note and my alibi, then I returned to the open till, which was empty.

I raised the alarm, the police were called and I was interrogated for two hours. They finally accepted my story once they had checked out my alibi, who had given me change from one of the other tills, but I was sure the police believed that I was in on it.

I promised myself that it would never happen again. But it was a good Christmas!

Jacko and me at Southend

Chapter 9

Life is changing very fast, I can't keep up. JFK, president of the US, got himself shot in the head. I remember the day, so vivid in my mind. The town centre was buzzing with silence; the people were walking around in a daze. There were dark clouds in the sky; it was quiet and eerie.

People liked him, I even liked him, his wife was young and beautiful – they gave hope to the world, a positive hope for the future. He had dealt with the Cuban missile crisis when we all thought that there was going to be a nuclear war. I was sure that was partly the reason for his death. And I remember that beautiful blonde film star, with those ruby red lips. She was found dead, an overdose of pills, drugs or something. Was that murder or suicide?

Not selling much on my fruit and veg stall today, things will never be the same since I gave Alfie £200 from the till. I really love my job, and I know they also love me. I am so happy here, I hope I won't have to leave.

I am meeting up with Jacko tonight, he has fixed me up with a date. He has got a regular girlfriend now and he doesn't want to share her, so she's bringing a friend along, Rosemary her name is. I am looking forward to the meet. I have asked my Mr Billings if I can leave twenty minutes early. "No problem," he said.

"How much money did you make today, Stephan?" he enquires.

"I'm not too sure, about £200." I almost choke on the words.

I am no longer allowed to keep more than £50 in the till, I have to take it into the main cash point. I can't really say that I blame them, it's a good idea, and now I have good reason not to set up a second robbery with Alfie and mum.

When I finish work I am going to buy myself some new shoes for tonight's date. Jacko also fixed me up with a date last week. She pulled a long thin knife on me when I tried to get into her knickers; she looked really scared and dangerous. Why did she agree to go to the bedroom and start kissing? I kept wondering at what point she would have used the knife, it was a long thin one like they use to open envelopes.

You need to be a bit of a psychologist when dating, it's a complex serious matter, and sometimes dangerous even. Jacko never seems to have any problems with girls, I am just learning as I go along, open to all experiences.

On one occasion Jacko took me to one of his neighbours' house, just two or three houses from where he lives with his family. It was on the corner, and what a weird, strange family they were! John, the boy, was two years older than Jacko and me, and his sister was even older. Apparently she used to be a nun. There was an old blind lady in the house; she kept walking around saying, 'Is that you, John? Is that you?' I don't really know why Jacko took me there, but it was a bizarre experience. John, the brother, had pulled down his sister's knickers and was trying to have sex with her – I couldn't believe my eyes – and the old lady going around calling out 'Is that you, John?' and everyone trying not to make any noise, and Jacko upstairs looking for the old lady's money. And me, as always, looking and trying to understand the how's and why's of people's lives.

Back at my veg stall, I finish twenty minutes early and rush off in search of shoes suitable for my date. I find what I'm looking for – two inch Cuban heels. Jacko told me she was a tall girl, those shoes would make me appear taller.

Rosemary was a bit shy and had little to say, but she was smart and clean, with long legs. She seemed secretive and deep, but I had little interest in her emotional needs, I just wanted to have sex with her.

I was set up now in my own little room at home with a lock on the inside of my bedroom door. I really wanted to take her home to my room and lock the door, just me and her alone to have sex together. She was clearly up to give it a try. I thought of the girl with the knife some days earlier, Rosemary doesn't look like the type to carry a knife, but how does one tell? Maybe I should have a look in her handbag or maybe I will just ask her how far did she want to go and does she carry a knife. But first we need to get home to my safe little room. Would my mum be home? How would I sneak her in and up the stairs? I will go in first and check out the situation. I knew it was risky but I was keen to test out my freedom and boundaries – the stakes were high.

All went well and soon I had Rosemary locked into my bedroom and on my bed with my hand up her skirt. She was loving it – I couldn't believe my luck! Then my mother started screaming and shouting, and the house started to tremble at the sound of her terrible voice. 'You fucking this' and 'you fucking that', I don't know who she was screaming at but I was thankful that it wasn't me. I knew it was disturbing for Rosemary; although she gave me no obvious signs, I could feel her uneasiness about the situation.

"I think it best if I go," she said.

I didn't want her to go, but my mother's screams were becoming more aggressive and embarrassing.

"Are you sure you want to go, she will stop soon," I said.

Ten minutes later there was no change. She was still screaming like a lunatic. Rosemary was clearly scared by the sounds of my mother's screams – I was even scared!

Outside my bedroom window there was a flat porch roof that one could stand on, above the front door, seven or eight foot from the ground. The drainpipe was fixed to the sidewall; I would often use this to exit from my bedroom, for me it was no problem, I would be out of the window and down the drainpipe in a flash. I felt that Rosemary would have little problem with her long, strong-looking legs.

"You will need to go down the drainpipe," I told her, "It's easy, I do it all the time. Get out onto the flat roof and then you can go down the pipe at the side."

She climbed out with no problem. She then reached out for the drainpipe but clearly lacked the confidence to take hold using handgrips only. I started to panic a bit now.

"Can you jump?" I said, desperate to resolve the situation. "Go on, jump. You'll be OK."

Once or twice it looked like she was thinking about it, but she just couldn't bring herself to take the leap. It was a long way down onto concrete. She tried the drainpipe again – no she wasn't going down that way.

"Jump, jump, go on!" I kept saying to her, "You'll be OK. I will see you in a couple of days." I gave her a little push and she was gone. I heard the thud as she landed on the concrete; she made no sound. I watched her as she walked away limping. I was relieved, and felt some pride in her; she was a tough girl, tougher than she gave herself credit for. I had not jumped from the roof myself, I always took the easier way, down the drainpipe. I liked girls that showed courage and physical strength.

We met up a few days later with Jacko and his girlfriend, and the four of us went over to the gravel pits. Rosemary was wearing black lace knickers and suspenders, she looked very sexy. It looked like my luck was in and she was going to let me have sex with her. My cock was rock hard, I got it up her and made about five or six hard thrusts then it was all over, I came up inside her. I had shot my load and had no concern for her needs or wants. She was clearly disappointed, and I just left her lying there, legs wide open, in her sexy black lace underwear that she had worn just for the occasion. I felt so unsure about the situation – that was the very first time that I had fully engaged in sexual intercourse – I clearly had a lot to learn. For me it was a memorable occasion, but I doubt very much that she was of the same mind. I think that the fact it was mid-day in open ground and other people walking around had not helped! She obviously wanted a good hard shag, but we never attempted to have sex again. I felt a little ashamed of my performance; Jacko was still at it.

It was clear to me that sex was a very important part of growing up – along with stealing motorbikes, getting money, buying stylish clothes and alcoholic drinks for the girls, robbing garages, banks and trains. If you don't have it, go and get it; nobody is going to come along and give it to you; be a man and go out and take a few risks; get noticed, create a bit of excitement, be in a gang and take care of each other; be strong, get respect for yourself, hide your shame, fear and insecurities. I don't need to read or write, I don't need any qualifications, I am young and the world belongs to me, I have many years to learn how to be in this world, I have nothing to fear, only fear itself.

I love my job so much. It gives me so much pleasure, everybody seems to like me, the customers are always giving me praise and asking after me. My job is so important, I feel like I belong. It gives me freedom and independence, self-respect. I can buy myself new clothes, which make me feel good, and I can still go horse riding when I choose. I can go home with pride and with money in my pockets.

But I rarely give my mother any money – she just wastes it. I am different and separate from my family, and no one ever need know the secrets of my shame and fear and guilt. I feel like a man now. I have two tattoos: on one arm a dagger and a snake, and on the other two hearts with 'mum' and 'dad' on them. I'd got drunk at the weekend with Jacko, we took some drugs, speed or something, I don't really know what it was. We ended up in central London in a tattoo shop, out of our heads.

Jacko has become a close friend now, we are loyal to each other, like brothers – I always wanted a brother. There are three others in the gang: Brian, Dobo, and

Dave. Brian is tall, about six foot six, and the rest of us are all shorter than normal, like pygmies. What a strange looking sight, I am sure! I think it makes Brian a little uneasy when it comes to fights, he is the one they go for first. We get into fights most weekends now.

Jacko is just a little shorter than me but he is stockier; his dad is big as he was a heavy-weight champion boxer and a docker. He wears his cap to one side. He's like my uncle Jack, really tough. I can't help wondering which one is the toughest. My uncle was said to be the hardest man in town.

Uncle Jack didn't like the army; he hated everything about it, and spent most of his National Service either on the run or locked up peeling spuds. He was very different from so-called normal people: he was intelligent and resourceful, fearless but careful; he couldn't read. Sounds a bit like me!

It's payday today and a night out with the boys. We're going to see Johnny Kid and the Pirates, a popular rock group. It should be a good night out with lots of girls on the dance floor to choose from. I am all dressed up and ready to go, eager and excited about what the night will bring.

We all set off on the bus together, a little bit noisy on the top deck. I tell the lady with the ticket machine I am not with that riffraff and request a cheaper fare, intending this as some kind of joke. She gave me the cheaper fare, but she was not happy about it. I thought that I was being funny and clever, apparently not as it turned out – she came back two stops later and asked me to leave the bus. I told her that I had changed my mind, and offered to pay more money. But she refused to accept it and, believing that I had not done anything wrong, I refused to leave the bus. So she called the police, which I felt was unnecessary, disrupting the trip. As far as I was concerned she was just a grumpy old cow with no sense of humour.

My mates didn't want to sit on the bus waiting for the police to turn up, they wanted to get to the dance; it was only one more stop down the road. I told them not to get involved.

"Go to the dance, I'll see you there later."

"OK," they said, and they went off, walking.

A big tall copper turned up, he must have been six feet six inches tall plus his helmet, which he had to take off to fit onto the top deck. He asked me to get off the bus, but I told him that I hadn't done anything wrong and refused to go – I had offered money to pay the full fare, and surely this was enough. It seemed to me that the real problem had been that the others were making too much noise, that's why I sat away from them.

The police officer informed the other passengers that he was entitled to use as much force as necessary to remove me from the bus. He then proceeded to take hold of my arm, with little effect. I was determined to stand by what I believed to be my right as a free person. I failed to see that I had done any wrong, I was out to enjoy myself not to cause harm – why were people in authority so serious and miserable about kids having fun and enjoying themselves?

But I was about to enter into realms beyond my understanding. The tall man in police uniform had a job to do, alone and observed by many people, a very awkward situation – no back up, no radio, and a very difficult and determined fifteen year old to deal with. His first and only intention was to remove me from the bus, as easily and as quickly as possible. My priority was to stay on the bus and keep face.

The policeman tried to force me off the bus and I took a knock to my head, which caused a nosebleed. It was at this point that I lost any understanding of the situation and something else from somewhere else kicked in – I now became the attacker and aggressor rather than the victim. I knocked his helmet to the floor and kicked it down the stairs, then punched him in the face. I felt a shift in me that scared me; I knew that this was very serious and I was in big trouble but powerless to change anything, the act was done and there was no going back. This moment would change the rest of my life – the true me had shown its head.

I could have resisted more but there was no need now, the situation was very different. Instead of the police officer trying to drag me off the bus, I was pushing him down the stairs and off the bus just as quick as I could. Maybe my intention was to run away from the situation, more than likely. We were now off the bus, it had stopped by a police phone box at the side of the road. The police officer took a tight hold of me with one hand and with the other grabbed the phone from the bus driver, who had called for help. The next thing I knew there were police cars coming from all directions.

Oh my God, what had I done? Things had gone terribly wrong – it wasn't meant to turn out this way. What is wrong with me, am I really so stupid? Why am I so stubborn and defiant?

Now I had six wild, crazy police officers to contend with. They bundled me into a car and sat on me. Thank God it was less than a five-minute journey to the station, I was struggling to breathe. They got me into one of the cells and then three of them proceeded to beat me up, wearing black leather gloves, one punch after another. The beatings from my mother had conditioned me for such a moment, but I now realised there was a new lesson to be learnt: 'time to grow up boy', as one of the officers said while laying into me.

Alfie turned up some hours later.

"What the fuck have you been doing to him?" he said when they opened the cell door. They told Alfie that I had knocked out one of the police officer's teeth. I didn't believe that.

I appeared at court some weeks later, and they were not happy with me as I was already on a two-year probation order for stealing a motorbike. What else did they know about me, I wondered, they must have known that I had run away from home when I was eleven, and that I had been locked up at fourteen for possession of drugs and not attending school.

I was convicted and remanded for reports at a young offenders centre. Normally it would be two weeks, but for some reason it had to be three. Good job they didn't know about me stealing a policeman's bicycle from outside the police station, and the garage I robbed, and the two hundred pounds taken from the till at my job. But then I couldn't help wonder if they did.

I went down the stairs from the dock to the cells below. How many times will I walk down these stairs over the next ten years, how many silent hours of thinking and waiting for the prison wagon to turn up? A long, hard day of thoughts and lonely inner sadness.

The wagon comes late into the afternoon, and off I go to the young offenders centre to the special block where they keep convicted boys. I was charged and convicted of ABH, which means actual bodily harm, or was it GBH? I don't really know – it all seemed so irrelevant.

What a shock I was in for, prison officers everywhere. They call the prison officers screws – I have no idea why, maybe it's the round flat heads caps they wear. I think most of them must have served their national service in the army.

It's difficult to find the words to describe my feelings when locked up inside a prison wagon, looking out of the very small windows trying to see where you are in the world. Not so much a physical street location, but more like a deep searching of one's soul, looking for understanding of one's emotional and spiritual ability. Searching my mind, trying to make some sense of how I felt. What was I doing wrong in my life, how did I get myself into this mess, how am I supposed to feel, and what am I expected to do about it?

How was I going to survive this terrible, scary situation – how long was it going to last? How would I deal with my fears and emotions, and the physical separation from my family and the outside world? I had no idea what to expect, and I was scared!

As a kid I had always seen myself as a loner, and very capable of enduring and surviving any situation on my own, but suddenly the reality of what it really felt like to be alone hit me, making me feel sick down to the core of my stomach. Until now I had had no idea how serious my problems were. I felt ill and very alone.

The barbed wire fence is everywhere, steel doors, and bars all around. The noise is disturbing – the clashing of steel gates clanging together, steel bolts and the constant turning of keys in locks. Everything is clean and spotless, shiny polished floors, with the smell of polish hanging in the air. Nobody speaks unless spoken to. Prison officers in uniforms and young boys in shabby prison clothes.

Some of the prisoners act like screws because they have been given a privileged job helping out with the strict systematic running of the reception area, with every moment controlled and watched by many eager eyes. Direct instructions – 'do this', 'do that', 'shut up', 'just answer my question' and 'do as you are told or you will be in big trouble'.

I failed to call the screw 'sir' when replying to a question. Bang, a hard slap around the head – I feel sick in my stomach. I suffer from severe migraine headaches and the horrible weak sickness that comes with them, but this is not the time or place to suffer from a migraine headache. I flash back to school and remember the times I would get hit around the head with a heavy book by one of the nasty female teachers, how I hated her and wanted to hit her back. The slap from the screw comes very quick without warning, almost unseen by anyone. My response is total silence, showing no emotions whatsoever.

"Just shut your mouth and do what you are told and you will be all right."

Strip off naked, give up all your clothes, open your legs astride, bend over and touch your toes, get in the shower, get out when you are told – two minutes after you washed with the water temperature just higher than cold. Dry yourself off, pick up your prison clothes, get dressed. Barely dried, go inside the cubicle, shut the door behind you, don't talk to anyone and listen for your name to be called out. No one dare speak, listening intently for names called out every fifteen or twenty minutes; we get taken away in groups of five or six at a time.

Off to the allocated cells set out on three levels on different wings or blocks. The young offenders wing is set apart from the other wings. Everywhere is very quiet and very clean; I like clean and quiet solitude. The screw has a card that holds all your personal details and on this card is your prison number, which you need to learn very quickly. Your card goes outside the cell to one side of the heavy steel door, which has a small spyhole in the centre at eye level that is used to look into the cell without the prisoners knowing. I follow along until my name is called.

"Sims!"

"Sir!" I reply without delay.

The door was opened with unnecessary force, noise and aggression. "In you go. Lights out in twenty minutes." The door slams shut.

Lights out in twenty minutes, and this is home for the next three weeks. Not long, it doesn't look too bad. My first concern is to get the bed made up before lights out. How long is twenty minutes?

I am exhausted by emotions. I look at the water jug and there is no water in it. It is a very strange feeling when you are locked in a room alone in the dark with no water – you are suddenly aware of the lack of any power or control you have over the situation. But that is the way it is, there is nothing to do but accept it. You become very conscious of the importance and value of water, and anyone who's been without water will know the fear associated with the lack of it.

Maybe I will be safe here, maybe their intentions are good, maybe they will take care of me, maybe the lack of water was a mistake and I will get some tomorrow. Surely I will survive one night without water. What do I do if I am ill or if there is an emergency – fire or something? Don't get ill, and trust that all will be well.

I lay there in the dark, thinking, looking up at the bars on the window and out beyond, up into the sky, searching for something beyond my thoughts, searching for courage and understanding, wisdom and knowledge from somewhere else. Things become very clear in a way I had never seen them before, a new experience, a new unknown fear of what tomorrow may bring.

Being locked up alone is tough. Morning comes very quickly, 5.30am, with a horrendous noise that I will never forget. What the fuck is that? Screams and shouts followed by steel doors being struck, kicked and banged on with wooden truncheons, door bolts rattled. This would happen every morning and last for thirty minutes.

My years at summer camp with the army cadets were about to pay off: my bedding was made up with perfection. I'm not going to give them a chance to pick on me, bedding boxed up: blanket, sheet, blanket, sheet, blanket, and no folds seen.

The door was flung open. I gave no signs of fear and panic, but slowly turned around to view the intruding force. I saw a long arm with a pointed finger directed towards my eyes. A voice shouted, "Get your bowl and get some water!" Simple, clear instructions. I grabbed my stainless steel bowl and moved towards the door, the tall ginger figure moved to one side as if to invite my exit. As I stepped out beyond the doorway I was struck hard on the side of my head, slap, which left ringing in my ears. The tall ginger figure took a step towards me and said in my ear, "Don't you ever come out of your cell without any shoes on."

I made no reply, but looked at him to see what I was dealing with. Was this his normal behaviour or was this just a one-off? Was I being deliberately singled out? I looked at him deeply: he was very ginger and very tall, the peak of his cap came down flat, shielding his eyes, and making him hold his head high in order to see out into the world at a 45 degree angle like a military guardsman. Yes, that's what he was – a guardsman. Not only was he a guardsman but, unknown to me, he was also the most feared prison PTI, physical training instructor, who I would be seeing every day for many months to come.

I will never forget that morning, there was so much information flashing through my mind. Two slaps within twelve hours. What did I need to understand here? This man has power and confidence; he is making a direct challenge to me. He has a job to do – he is getting paid to do it by the government. He has authority, a truncheon at his side with authorisation to use it at his own discretion; he has work colleagues that will come running to his aid in numbers and within seconds of his request if and when he needs it; he is strong and fit, trained, experienced and skilful. He has twice my years of knowledge, a physical training instructor, guardsman, years of military service and training. Would I be so bold and stupid to accept his challenge? What would I have to offer: fifteen years old and what do I know? And what have I learnt about life that would give me any chance of success?

Or will I claim to know everything? He can't tell me anything I don't already know. I've already been and done it and got the T-shirt. I know it all and I am not afraid of anything or anyone.

Actually, I am a lost, fearful and vulnerable child. I will not surrender myself to any foolish traps of ego. He knows that I can see into him, and he knows that I am not a fool, though I'm only fifteen years. This moment will pass and only I will be the victim of it and it will never go unforgotten.

I turn away and place my shoes on my feet; I will never leave my cell again without shoes as requested – as commanded. For this I thank him. He is gone now; I take my bowl and go for water, hot water.

There are many comings and goings, no one talks. I watch for simple learnings – where they go to, and be sure to know the way back. What is the hot water for, what is the aluminium jug for? I need to be sure that I know my personal prison number and cell number. I return safely to my cell – it quickly becomes clear to me that the cell is the only place of safety that one has here, it is my very special personal space, if I keep it clean and do as I am told all will be ok. Don't answer back, and call every officer 'sir'. It occurred to me that I had not addressed the PTI as 'sir'. I wonder why he had let it go. I must make a point of calling him 'sir' next time he confronts me, he will be waiting for me to address him correctly.

The cell door slams tightly, closed hard with a bang. Everything here is done with a hard noisy slam, all locks and bolts, doors and steel gates are done with a slam and bang, a slam and bang that I will always remember.

I take a wash in the now warm water of the steel bowl. I still have no drinking water in my jug. I inspect the jug, it has a smell that I am not familiar with, not a very pleasant smell, there are green barnacle-type things stuck to the bottom, I don't know what they are, but clearly they have been there for some time.

I must get some drinking water next time the cell door is opened. The warm water gives me a sense of well-being, I feel clean. I now know where the water is and when to get it, but I am still very much aware that I might be in for a hard time. I feel very uneasy about the situation, unsure and afraid. I feel that I'm not liked, uncertain as to my ability to deal with it, not really knowing what it is that I have to deal with.

The next time the cell door is opened it is the call to go for breakfast in the main hall down the stairs on the ground floor. The prison is buzzing with activity, hundreds of prisoners all wanting to be fed, dozens of screws trying to keep discipline and control. This is where everyone talks at the same time. This is where conflict happens.

I've always found the sound of many human voices scary and overwhelming. I find it difficult to understand the need to make constant conversation. What are they talking about? Is it really so important and necessary to talk about what they have done and what they have been, stories, jokes, egos. 'I am this', 'I am that', 'who are you?' It all comes out of fear and need: the need to feel safe, egos to contend with, the need to belong, to be accepted. 'Please like me', 'please respect me', 'accept me'. If you don't like or accept me then you must respect me; if not, the only other alternative is to fear me.

I don't think anyone really wants to be in a hostile, violent, dangerous environment. That's really scary, and this is the scariest place on earth that I know of. I feel so childlike and powerless; I think I need to toughen up a bit.

The most dangerous times are meal times, and slopping out first thing in the morning, when everyone comes out of their cells buzzing with resentment and fear. This is when most fights and violence happen. When the food is being served out there is a very high level of eye contact and very few words. Then suddenly there are extreme acts of violence with intent to severely harm and no consideration of the consequences.

The second day I was there I watched intently when a fight broke out between two guys at the next table. Most prisoners were between eighteen and twenty years old, three or four hundred of them in total, with about fifty young offenders like myself. We all watched with delight as these two guys threw punches at each other across the table, each punch with maximum intent to cause injury.

As soon as it started, without warning, two screws set about them with truncheons. The two guys responded with a level of violence I had never seen before. The metal dinner trays that we all ate from were used like weapons, eighteen inches by twelve with thin-ridged edges like swords – a good strike could cut your head off if enough force was used. One of the prison officers took the full force across his nose; blood spurted out everywhere as he fell to the floor.

On every table there was a large aluminium teapot that had three or four litres of boiling hot tea, always piping hot – too hot to drink. One of the blokes picked up the teapot and threw it into the face of the other prison officer; he stumbled away screaming. The doors to the hall were quickly locked from the outside and the kitchen was locked down. All the remaining screws were locked in with the prisoners. Twenty screws were quick to take control, some going to the aid of the fallen officers and most of the rest going to secure and remove the two attacking prisoners, six on each one, with vicious and controlled action. I would not like to be on the receiving end of an attack from these guys. If you resisted then they would be willing to kill you if it was necessary for the safety of their buddies. If they were not willing to back each other then they could be in big trouble.

The two guys were quickly taken away – God knows what happened to them. If they survived they would not be seeing the light of day for a very long time. The whole thing shocked me: the way the two prisoners were able to carry out such a violent act on the two screws, and the effectiveness of the prison officers in containing the situation, which could have quickly escalated into something far more serious. I was surprised by the viciousness of both sides; the ruthlessness and consequences were extreme. It was clear to me that the prison officers had been well trained for such an event, dangerous and volatile, the speed at which everything was controlled and suppressed amazed me.

I thought on it for many days. There were four times every day when the potential for similar violence was possible. Slop out, breakfast, dinner, and evening meal times were highly charged. I don't know who was worse, the screws or the prison inmates. I guess it was us against them, and them against us.

I don't like it here – it's not for me! I just want to get out and get back home. Back to my job on the fruit and veg stall, back to the safety of my little room and my family. In a strange way I even miss the screams and shouts of my mother. But for now I am stuck here, and I need to deal with it, one day at a time.

Reality soon strikes home. The young offenders are subjected to physical training every day, and I will start tomorrow. Then I will meet up with the tall ginger PTI guardsman again, notorious and feared, for one and a half hours of non-stop, unrelenting physical exercise. Don't talk and don't be last or you will be punished. Surely it can't be that bad, I'm fit and strong enough to compete against the other lads – I'm no fucking wimp – I may not be tall but I'm strong, resourceful and determined.

Tomorrow comes and I'm ready, eagerly waiting, dressed in vest and shorts, and black prison plimsolls, no socks, listening for noises in the quietness, that may give warning of any activity.

We are not allowed to lie on our beds during the day. This makes life a little difficult, so I've taken to lying on the floor sometimes. Either you stand up and walk around, backwards and forwards across the cell floor, approximately ten foot long by seven foot wide, or sit down at the small wooden chair and desk. There's little or nothing to read and nothing to write with. What are you supposed to do in such a situation? Strange and harsh, I can make little sense of it, other than to assume that the intention is to cause suffering and hardship.

I constantly look up to the window, out to the sky and beyond. Is it morning or afternoon; day or night; cloudy, rain, or sunshine? If I stand on the chair and go up on my toes I can just see out over the windowsill, out to the high barbed-wire fences. But if the screws catch you looking out you're in for a bollocking: you're not allowed to look out of the window; the chair is for sitting on, not for standing on.

It's really tough here, but in a strange kind of way I approve and get a weird kind of sense of order and sureness about how things should be – simple, clean, tidy, and orderly.

I hear voices spoken, cell doors opening; I can hear a strange quietness looming outside my cell door. The door opens; the prison officer gives orders; I take a quick look before I move out. The other boys are forming up in two lines along the corridor. I see the ginger PTI coming and slam my cell door behind me and join the other boys. I speak to no one. There is one other PTI with dark hair, younger and shorter with bulging chest and arm muscles.

Off we go, running down the corridor.

"Get your knees up!" the ginger guardsman screams out. Then the second muscle-bound PTI comes alongside.

"Get your knees up!" he commands with the authority of the ginger guardsman.

Down the stairs go about twenty of us boys – fifteen, sixteen, seventeen years old. At the bottom of the stairs we turn left.

"Get those knees up and keep them up!"

Every time a steel gate is opened we have to run on the spot. We go through and the gates are locked behind us, Ginger at the front and Muscles at the rear, into the passageway that runs under the prison.

"OK, who spoke?" Ginger stops us, but we keep running on the spot.

"Who spoke?" he said again. "OK, down you go, bunny hop position."

Everyone squats down, bent knees, up on our toes. I take the same position and off we go bunny hopping all the way to the gym – about a hundred yards. I soon learn that this was a regular procedure every day. No one ever spoke – they wouldn't dare, they would get beaten up by the other boys if they did. Ginger was known as Bunny Hop Hooper. He had us hopping everywhere. We arrived at the gym and everyone was knackered, but no one was allowed to stop or rest. No one ever spoke and if you were last you were punished. Someone always had to be last – it was his clever way of keeping us at maximum speed with maximum effect.

Thank God for the weak fat boys! There were always one or two fat boys that fell behind and they suffered for it. But it wasn't quite that simple, the PTIs were always looking for any reason to single out one of the rest of us. I was punished only once, I didn't ever know what I did wrong, but I got twenty push ups, which I struggled to do, trying to do every single push up perfectly as everyone was watching me whilst they ran on the spot. I never got caught out again.

I now knew what PT stood for – physical torture. The large main doors to the gym were opened and outside into the yard we hopped. It was a heat wave summer, very high temperatures, and we went out into the blazing sun, which initially we felt extremely grateful for. But thirty minutes later it became a serious problem for everyone, except the PTIs that is!

I don't think I'd seen anyone cry before, a grown person I mean, maybe I saw Alfie cry once. I don't even recall seeing my sisters cry, but this day I saw two boys cry, and others that were very near to tears. This place is the last place you want to be seen crying. In a strange sort of way it made me feel safe and gave me an odd kind of comfort: I was terrified of being seen to cry, but there was no chance of that, even though I was really scared and suffering physically. My tongue began to swell up and I was finding it difficult to get enough air into my lungs. I don't think that I could have gone on for much longer, maybe that's what I feared most.

We went back inside the gym, but it was far from over: up on the wall bars, hanging there, leg raises, up and down; pull ups using our arms to pull ourselves up and down. This went on for another 10 or 15 minutes and then we hopped all the way back to our cells. No shower. I was exhausted and I would do this every day except Sundays. It was a really scary thought and I would think about it all day and all night: the anticipation of tomorrow and the next day, and every day after – never ending. This was going to be a part of my daily life; I needed to find a way to adjust, and accept it without too much fear and trauma. And very quickly I somehow came to accept that horrible feeling inside me, though I neither enjoyed it nor looked forward to it.

But after a couple of weeks of this routine I felt much more confident in myself, and in my body and mind. I felt strong, and capable of surviving Bunny Hop Hooper. He would find a way to make us struggle and suffer; he was clearly good at his job, he knew what he was doing and got a great deal of pleasure from it.

I noticed that he never made eye contact with me. Why was this? I knew that he was watching me, he always knew where I was and what I was doing, but he would never make eye contact with me – not from that very first day when he gave me a slap around the head for coming out of my cell without shoes on.

The weeks soon passed; there was a lot to think about whilst locked up in the cell, alone and in silence day after day. Thinking about court: what would the report say about me; what would the punishment be; would they let me go home? I had surely learned a lesson that I would remember for the rest of my life. So there is no reason to punish someone if they have learnt a lesson from it, is there?

I am a better person now, I feel more positive, and hopefully I can see where I am at in my life. I sure don't ever want to come back here again. This is a place to come just for a short while, just to find out that being free outside in the world is a blessing, where one can know the real value of freedom and choice. Family, friends, work, money, going out, buying clothes, girls, clubs, dancing, drinking, just walking; learning how to be a man, and so much more to do and be.

I wondered what the court would read and learn about me, what would they know of me. Can't read or write, no qualifications, adopted, a German bastard child of a bomber pilot, ran away from home and stole a policeman's bike, beat up my girlfriend, robbed the garage – they already know about me stealing a motorbike – stole £200 from the till at the place I loved to work, the place where everybody loved me, and now a violent attack on a police officer. Will they know that I killed Carl, my mum's cat, my uncle's canary? Will they know that I hate my mother and that I blackmailed her as a child?

There is a deep raging pain somewhere inside that sometimes scares the shit out of me. Am I in big trouble? Do I need help? Am I sick? And this other thing in me that I know and I trust looks after me – my angel, the light – is it real or not?

What am I to tell the court next week – will I tell them anything about my problems and feelings? I just can't see me saying anything. I could tell them what happened on the bus, tell them how I feel about it all and how it came about. I didn't do anything wrong! Why should I get off the bus? I offered to pay. I was just standing by what I thought was right. I find it difficult to handle the injustice of it. Why would I tell the court this? Why would I not? Will it make any difference? And maybe I am guilty as charged, regardless of circumstances. The police officer was just trying to do his job; and I am just trying to be in the world, just trying to learn how to belong in it. I am trying to grow up into a man; I must have faith in truth and justice.

I have so much to think about. I look up to the sky just as I did in my pram as a very small child – those magical walks to the park with my nan, looking up through the branches. I am full of deep sorrow and sadness; I have no idea where it comes from and I have even less idea what to do about it.

Life moves on, stopping for no one,
sorrow nor tears will bring it to slow.
If you fail to take adequate learning
you will fall and drop to the ground
and be trampled by many.
There is no discrimination,
it is good advice not to be
fooled by names and words.
Be sure to take the time to learn well
the lies and trickery in people's words.

Chapter 10

I say nothing, just listen. They tell me that they have read the reports and given a great deal of time and thought as to the best way to deal with me, as they put it.

"We have decided that you will go to a detention centre for a period of six months, and we trust we won't see you again. Is there anything you wish to say before you go down?" When they say 'go down' they mean go down the stairs to the cells – you always go down the stairs from the courtroom.

I gave no reply, turned away and went down the stairs showing no concern or fear. How could I let them know that I was terrified and wanted to go home, back to my family and my four sisters and my friends? I hadn't meant to do it and I shall not be doing it again.

I waited in the cells all afternoon for the prison wagon. Back to Ashford for processing, I will have lots of time to think now, six months. Back to Ashford Remand Centre, the young offenders unit in Middlesex. I know what to expect now when arriving at the reception block, but I am even more scared than I was the first time. Do all the other lads feel the same way when they come here? I guess they must do, but different blokes deal with it in different ways I suppose.

Different cell now, same block. I feel more sure of myself, I know what to do in the morning. Slop out, empty your piss pot, a horrible plastic pot stained with brown urine from many past months and years; if you got a lid you were lucky. What a horrible smell it gives, a kind of ammonia that takes your breath away if you are too near.

I have to go to the processing wing for the first week of my sentence and they tell me that there is a waiting period of about three months, so I will stay at Ashford until a vacancy comes.

I have been allocated to the detention centre at Send and I've heard bad stories about it. You get PT twice a day, run everywhere, no talking, all the screws are like Bunny Hop Hooper the guardsman. This place is said to be a picnic compared to Send so I best be thankful and get settled in. They give me a job cleaning the shower and toilets, and scrubbing the floors. I'm allowed to work on my own and no one bothers me, I get paid enough money to buy some tobacco.

But I still have to do PT everyday with Bunny Hop Hooper. I am beginning to enjoy it now in a strange, fearful way – I don't think the idea was to make it enjoyable. Ginger has still never acknowledged me, and never makes eye contact with me; there was only one time he acknowledged me and called me by my name. One day we had set off as usual, knees up high. "Who spoke?" he said. I put my hand up high in the air, I don't really know why I did it, I just wanted to challenge the idea in some way. The rest carried on running, and I had to hop all the way on my own. I was knackered when I got there as always, but this time everyone else was fresh. It was all I could do to keep up and keep myself from being last, with more punishment. The ginger guardsman spoke quietly in my ear on the way back, "No good being a martyr in this place, Sims." He was right. I never did it again, but it was an experience that I would always remember.

I received a letter from my job saying how much they missed me and they were sorry but they would have to let my job go. It was good of them to write to me.

I spent my sixteenth birthday in Ashford Remand Centre. Strange, they never did send me off to the detention centre. I did four months at Ashford, and lots of thinking, and lots of PT. I grew six inches and gained a stone of sheer muscle; I was fit and strong. I wouldn't have any chance of being a jockey now.

After four months they let me go home: back to my family, and my little room that I missed so much, and my four sisters who I also missed, especially the youngest one, she was so pretty. All my sisters loved me and even Marie had a special kind of respect for me now. And my mother had changed towards me as well. I got myself a job with Jacko on a building site. They were building a block of flats; we dug out the foundations with a pick and shovel, hard work, all through the winter. It was cold and we started at 7.30am every morning. We were always keen and on time – they liked that!

Alfie came home from work one day, he was a paint sprayer now at a local factory that built portable timber-framed buildings.

"I've got you a job if you want it," he said, "as a carpenter and joiner. You will need to serve an apprenticeship for three years and go to college three days a week and one evening after work." I couldn't believe my luck. Alfie always seemed to know how to get things done.

I started work two weeks later, attending college as an apprentice carpenter and joiner. Just one problem I hadn't yet considered – I found it difficult to read and write. I was very slow and this was going to be a massive problem.

I started the job at the factory. They put me with another boy and we shared a carpentry bench together; I had one side and he the other. He was seventeen and had been there for one year and was going to college in his second year. He was very different from me in every way and was out to give me a hard time, and he did. I found it extremely difficult to make conversation with him; he was very chatty with everyone and always criticising my work. I found this humiliating and quickly grew to hate him, he really made my day hell. I would have been much better with an older person that I could learn from.

College was even more of a nightmare. I was even more terrified than being locked up at Ashford Young Offenders Centre, there at least I had my own space, did PT every day and didn't have to talk to anyone. The college was very different, everyone wanted to talk, and everyone was better than everyone else. This was a place of numbers, and the written word, reading and writing. Even though the first year was practical, there was lots of theory, talking, listening and reading what was written up on the board. I had to somehow write it down in my exercise book.

Normal boys would read one sentence and write it down in their books. I would look two or three times just to write one word. Everyone finished, the tutor would wipe off everything written on the board, and I had only managed to write half of it if I was lucky. When it came to re-write it in a way that I could understand I was not even able to read my own handwriting. I was terrified of being found out by the other boys; I was scared of being labelled as thick or stupid; terrified of being called names like I was at school, of not belonging, of being different from them. I didn't want to fight them like I always did, no backing, just them and me.

I had to deal with my problems alone and had no one to talk too. Every day was a struggle but I really tried hard to deal with it. The boy I worked with was relentless in his ways. I had to tell him that if he persisted in his form of bullying, I was going to punch his fucking face in. I am sure that he went to the office and complained; and then one of the older boys, one of his mates, kept giving me the stare at lunch breaks.

I made no friends at college and tried to keep myself to myself. I was very good at the practical side of work, probably better than most of the other boys, but when it came to theory, reading and writing I was under a great deal of stress trying to keep up, and to hide my fear and disability. It wasn't easy.

One day one of the tutors singled me out in front of the whole class. I had no idea what it was about. I found his aggression too much to handle, he was making me look stupid. My suppressed feelings came out and I was taken over with rage and fear, out of control. I stood up, grabbed his tie, wrapping it around my fist and pulling him towards me, and screamed into his face,

"You ever talk to me like that again and I will smash your fucking face in!" Then I let him go and walked out of the classroom.

Where did the rage come from? I think that I was as much scared of my rage as I was of people and of humiliation and persecution. I hated to be publically criticised, and did not know how to deal with it.

I went back to work on Monday; they called me into the office and told me that the college had been in touch, they told me that I would have to pack all my tools and go, there was nothing that could be done. I was devastated. What was I going to tell Alfie? He would be very disappointed with me.

I packed my tools away into the carpenter's toolbox that I had made at college. It was a test item and I got full marks on it; I loved my tools, every single one of them. I had to carry my toolbox all the way home, about four miles. I would climb over the fence at the army barracks. I cut through the barracks every day, as it took about a mile off the journey, but normally I had nothing to carry. This time I had my toolbox, full of tools and very heavy. I had to get it over the gates, about eight foot high they were. I must have been crazy – why did I have to do everything different from every one else?

I managed to get my toolbox up on top of the gates. I balanced it there while I climbed over myself, but in doing so the box of tools fell off and split – my pride and joy broken. It would be years before I fully repaired that box. I managed to struggle out of the army camp without being seen, arriving home exhausted and depleted.

I think I must have fallen into a deep depression. I didn't come out of my room for days; Alfie wasn't speaking to me; my mum asked what happened, I wasn't speaking to her. In fact I think at some level I felt that it was her who was responsible for my unbearable way of life. Fucking bitch, I felt like telling her to fuck off with her boyfriend. It was a long time before I came to terms with my loss.

I soon took up drinking and smoking. I started drinking in the daytime – not a good idea. I would buy half a bottle of rum or brandy or whatever it was – I think I tried them all. I would drink the bottle empty, have a sleep and then go out drinking again at night with Jacko and the gang. This would go on for weeks and months.

I got friendly with a woman I met at a party one night. I pushed her up against the wall and said, "I would love to fuck you," and she replied, "Why don't you come round tomorrow and give it a try." I spent the whole day in bed with her, I had six orgasms; she showed me everything I didn't know about sex. She was married with three children and thirty-five years of age. I was sixteen coming up seventeen.

I think that I must have gone to her house every day, having sex with her while her husband was at work and the children at school. This lasted about five or six weeks. What the hell was I doing? I knew that it was dangerous and wrong. I just couldn't get enough sex – I was a horny bastard. I knew somehow that it had to stop before her husband found out, and he did. He came looking for me one day; he said to my mum that he needed to speak to me. I never went there again, and he never came back.

I started back to work with Jacko on a building site. Jacko was always getting me jobs, there were so many jobs about, especially in the construction business; they were building everywhere. We were hod-carrying now, carrying bricks up ladders onto scaffolding for the bricklayer to use. This was a very demanding job, one had to be very fit and strong, with stamina. Myself and Jacko were always hard-working and we were respected for it.

I now spent more time with Jacko and the gang, more time drinking and playing snooker at the local snooker hall. Getting alcohol never seemed to be a problem, and sometimes we even managed to drink in pubs, insisting that we were eighteen and would bring ID next time. I was seventeen now, I loved being in a gang, I felt safe; these were my friends and they seemed to like me and understand me, I felt that I belonged somewhere.

I made up my mind I was going to pass my driving test and get myself a car. I started having driving lessons. I took to it very quickly, and very soon I was taking my driving test, which I failed because the handbrake cable of the car I was driving broke on a three-point turn so I couldn't complete the test. But it wasn't long before I was back again and this time I passed with flying colours. This was to change my whole way of life.

I remember going to the car auctions and buying my first car for £50. It was an old Austin Cambridge, I loved it, it was a solid 4-door, grey colour and Alfie was well impressed. I think he had now forgiven me for losing my job as a carpenter and joiner. I started buying and selling cars; every car I bought, I sold and doubled my money. It was great and it empowered me. I also had a new girlfriend now, Janet, my first real girlfriend. Up until now I had not really taken girls seriously, they were silly and just something to be used and abused, quick shag and move onto the next one. What a strange attitude to have, but it seemed to me that's how it was with most of the lads – don't get too involved with girls, shag 'em and leave 'em. The culture I grew up in was fight, fuck, and thieve – it was known as the three Fs.

I knew how to work, I knew how to make money, drink, shag, steal. Fights every Friday and Saturday nights, down town drinking, looking for girls, always ready for a fight, and on the way home at the end of the night go stealing until the early hours of the morning, steal anything worth taking home. One night I stole a motorbike with a sidecar, I took it home, a 350 BSA. It didn't occur to me that I was hurting anyone or doing anything wrong – I got a buzz from it. To me it was a normal part of growing up and being a man, just make sure you don't get caught, I didn't want to go back inside again. Unaware I was developing a serious drink problem, like everyone else I thought that in order to be a man one must be seen to be able to drink.

I haven't managed to have sex with Janet yet, she is putting up some resistance, but I have managed to get her into the sanctuary of my little bedroom. I am working on her.

I've got a new job with Marie's boyfriend at the dye works, a poxy job but it pays well, it will do me for a short while. One day at tea break my sister's boyfriend laughed when I put money in the tea machine and no cup came down, just the tea flowing down the back into the machine. He thought it was really funny, and looking back on it now it was, but I took offence and knocked him down to the ground.
"Don't fucking laugh at me!" I said.
He offered no resistance.

How strange of me to behave in such a way with a friend who clearly didn't mean any harm. If he had retaliated I was ready to hurt him without question or consideration of the consequences. I thought about it for weeks after and found my feelings and behaviour worrying: it seemed to me that I was changing – becoming more violent, aggressive, and dangerous with every day.

I am answerable to no one, I have no regular routine, the only thing going for me is that I am eager and willing to work. I watch, listen, and learn. I just love to learn how to do things, learning is worth much more than the payment I receive for doing the job. I am drinking every night and sometimes in the day. I am getting into trouble every week and have no idea how serious my problems are becoming. I am just trying to learn how to be a man and feel safe, to belong. How I long to feel safe and belong, unafraid.

It was not long before I found myself back in court.

Chapter 11

The court has remanded me for medical reports this time. They want me to be assessed by a psychiatrist, before passing sentence and punishment.

What the fuck am I doing back here?!

"Fall in for the film," the screw shouts out as he unlocks the cell door. What a racket as the prisoners form up along the corridor; I get in line making no sound.

"Shut up you noisy lot!" the screw screams. All goes so very quiet; you could hear a pin drop. A voice comes up from somewhere inside me.

"Bollocks!" it calls back to the screw. Deafening silence all around me. The screw turns and looks straight back at me; he points his finger to my face.

"You! Bang yourself up," he screams. 'Bang yourself up' means go back to your cell and slam the door shut behind you. I clearly won't be going to see the film now. I obey his orders and make back towards my cell. I need to pass him on the walkway and as I pass him he kicks me up the backside with his right foot. It didn't hurt me, but it shook me deep inside and something snapped: a rage such as I have never experienced before comes out and shows itself – a murderous feeling. It's terrifying; I really feel that I want to kill him.

I stop and turn back to face him. I look him square in the eyes. I seem to be somewhere else now, not really in my body. I grab him by his jacket lapels with both hands and slam him up against the wall. I stare hard into his eyes searching for something. What am I searching for? The other prison officers are unable to see him or me, as we are in a small recess now. If they could see me I would be in big trouble: they would sound the alarm bells and the screws would come running from all directions to rescue their colleague. It was a strange and powerful moment, I was full of fear and the officer was paralysed by his fear, unable to move, unable to reach for his whistle, unable to reach for his truncheon, unable to call out. It was all I could do to stop myself from head butting him in the face – I so much wanted to smash his face in. He must have sensed my dangerous feelings towards him. I got really close up to his face, almost lifting him off the floor.

"You ever touch me again and I will fucking kill you, you fucking bastard cunt!" I spurted out into his face, then let go of him and walked back to my cell slamming the door behind me.

What the fuck have I done? I'm in for a good beating now! I didn't know if I should make or find a weapon to defend myself with, or just take the beating that everyone gets if they ever touch one of the prison officers. I am really scared. I've done it now, I am in real big shit trouble now.

I wait. The prisoners go off to the film and I fearfully await my beating, not knowing how I'll respond to it. Ten minutes pass by. I hear voices, chains and keys rattling. They're coming – this is it. I choose to face them, with no weapon. The cell door is flung open with force, two screws standing there.

"Pack your kit up, you're going over to the hospital," they shout.

Was this some kind of a trap they had set for me? I'm beginning to believe that everyone and everything is against me – even God. Where is this fucking all-powerful and just, loving, wonderful God they speak of? I have no need of this God, I have myself to trust in. I see their deception and their pathetic needs and wants, and their denial of love and compassion. I will not be fooled so easily. But I did as I was told, accepting that I was at their mercy and must be willing and man-enough to surrender to their will and demands.

I quickly pack all my belongings into a pillowcase – this was the normal procedure to transport one's belongings around the prison, you were only allowed the amount you could fit into a pillowcase plus what you could carry or fit into your pockets. You had to be ready to move from one cell to another at a moment's notice. I waited in my cell with the door still open, two screws standing there.

"Sims."

"Yes, sir," I replied.

"Come with us, you are going over to the hospital."

Off we went. I was feeling very uneasy about the situation, I was still expecting to get a beating at some stage when they were ready for me. I expected the screw that I had attacked earlier to appear with his mates and truncheons at the ready.

Ten minutes later we arrived at the hospital block. This block was even more secure than the main block; the two screws handed me over with my personal details and paperwork. I was left in the charge of two medical officers.

"Take these tablets, they will help you." Reluctantly I took the tablets.

"Come with us," they said. These guys had a certain look about them that made me feel even more unsure, they seemed harder and insensitive. I followed them down the corridor.

"In you go," they said. The door was slammed behind me.

I felt cold, scared and alone. Maybe I wasn't going to get a beating, but I certainly wasn't going to be the most popular kid on the block. What the fuck are they going to do with me? The best thing I can do is make my bed up and see if I can get some sleep. Tomorrow's another day; maybe I just need to count my blessings, so far I have been very lucky.

So it's reports and back to court – what will they say about me? Why am I the way I am? What's wrong with me? I will destroy the very thing that I need, the thing that I want most – self-sabotage. I will test things until they break. I just want to feel safe and loved, I just want to feel accepted, to feel that I belong in the world. I don't really want much, but it seems impossible for me to have it.

I fall asleep; I am exhausted. I sleep all the way through until morning. I wake, not really sure where I am, asking myself: How did I get here? Was it all real or was it just a bad dream? Then I remember: medical reports – maybe they think I am nuts. Maybe I am nuts! Maybe I am in bigger trouble than I thought I was.

I hear some strange noises, screams and shouts. This is the nutters' wing, sounds like there's some really crazy, dangerous people in here. It's a good job they are locked up, I thought to myself. What am I to trust in now? I look around the cell for something that may give me comfort.

A screw comes to the cell door and speaks through the open hatchway.

"You'll be seeing the psychiatrist today," he tells me.

"OK," I reply.

"Dr Mary Ellis her name is."

"OK."

I felt some comfort in her being a woman. A female in this crazy male-dominated hell-hole – she must be brave or special, or maybe both.

Breakfast is brought to the cell door and passed in through the hatchway; I don't need to leave my cell, and I am allowed to lie down on the bed. This is great, soft and easy, not so hard and scary – except for the other inmates that is – and of course the screws all walking around in their white coats. Maybe I will be safe here. How many more days is it now before I go back to court? Sometimes I get a weird scary feeling inside me, a fear of never being let out again, locked in forever. I find the fear and the feeling of powerlessness lonely and overwhelming; I feel close to panic. I must be strong and fearless, in control of my feelings and emotions. I just want to get out of this place and back to court. What am I doing here? I don't belong here.

Later in the afternoon I am let out of my cell. They take me into an adjoining building. I see flowers on table-tops and pictures on the walls, I sense a different kind of energy – it feels safer.

"Sit down," the screw told me. He knocked on a door; there was a nameplate – Dr Mary Ellis – and then some letters after the name. A voice from behind the door calls out 'enter'; the screw opens the door.

"Mr Sims, ma'am." He turns to me, "In you go."

I move into the room, red carpet on the floor, a big wide desk and a grey-haired woman wearing glasses sat at the other side of the desk. I think she would be about fifty or may be even sixty years old.

"Sit down, Stephan," she tells me, there's a small chair with soft leather seating. "Is your name Stephen or Stephan?" she asks.

"Stephan," I reply.

"Sims, is that right?"

"Yeah."

"Well it seems you have got yourself into a bit of a mess, haven't you?"

"Yeah."

"What do you want to tell me about it?"

"I don't know, do you mean yesterday or outside, back home?"

"Back home."

"I was drunk at the time," I replied.

"You were drunk. Do you get drunk very often?"

"Not really."

"So why did you get yourself drunk on the day when you stole the Jaguar car?"

"I don't really know, I was out with my sister's boyfriend, he was older than me, eighteen, and he wanted to go into the pub for a drink so I just went along with him."

"Are you old enough to drink?"

"Not really."

"And what is it that you normally drink?"

"Brandy," I said, sounding very sure of myself.

"And this was about midday, was it?"

"Yeah."

"Then what happened?"

"We left the pub and went for a walk."

"So when did you take the car, soon after leaving the pub?"

As I sat there I was trying to see into her. What shall I tell her? Is she for me or against me? What difference will it make at court? Shall I tell her the truth or not? I am not sure that I know what the truth is! I don't really know what to say. She keeps asking questions. I feel safe with her and I feel that she is intelligent and understanding. Maybe this will be a good time to speak up.

"So why did you make off with the car?" she asked, looking straight into me, as if to insist on a true answer. I didn't really know what to say. I flashed back to that day. Why did I take the car? I hadn't really thought about it before. It was hot and sunny, there was the beautiful Jaguar car, the windows were open and the keys were in the ignition. It just seemed the right thing to do. What an opportunity! I was excited at the thought of driving this beautiful car at high speed. It seemed like an invite I couldn't refuse. I opened the door, got in and turned the key, revved up the engine, put it in gear and roared off down the street. My sister's boyfriend just managed to get in before I sped off, zigzagging down the road.

I had not expected the immediate response of power and speed. I was excited by the sheer rush of something that put me on a high – the feeling of being alive, and full of joy. Adrenalin – yes, it was adrenalin. I was alive, filled with excitement by my act of doing. As the Jaguar snaked down the road at speed it clipped a bus and a Post Office delivery van, which all added to the excitement.

"It seemed the right thing to do at the time," I said, leaving out the details of the excitement.

"So what about the road block and the policeman you almost killed?"

"The policeman tried to get into the car whilst it was still moving, and it was only going very slow. He tripped and fell as he tried to get into the car."

"It made big headlines in the newspapers – Stolen Car Drags Policeman," she said.

"I haven't seen the newspapers, and it was very much dramatized by the police – all lies and drama – trying to make themselves out as heroes."

"I see from your records that you were also involved in an act of violence with six police officers some weeks earlier. What was all that about?" she asks.

"They were beating up a man," I said, "they were hurting him badly. It was totally unnecessary."

"You were charged with three acts of assault on police."

"All lies," I replied, "I was the only one that was assaulted.

"And the damage you did to the police station," she asks.

"It seemed the right response for the injustice," I replied, I didn't know what else to say to her.

"The police officer on the bus, what about him?"

"I hadn't done any wrong, he got violent with me and I responded accordingly and got beaten up by three police officers at the police station, and I was punished for it, six months locked up."

She was silent and just looked at me for a while, motionless.

"Tell me about your childhood."

"Not much to tell really. I didn't go to school much, have a problem with reading and writing, no qualifications, don't get on with my mother very well, got four sisters and a step-dad. I was locked up at fourteen, kicked out of college, lost my job as a carpenter. I did try to join the Army before I got into trouble stealing the car, but they didn't want me due to the fact that I wasn't good at reading, and didn't know my times tables and ABC. He told me to come back in six months time."

"What's the worst thing you have ever done?" she said. This question stopped me dead in my tracks. I tried not to show any emotions. What shall I tell her? Shall I tell her that I killed Carl? Shall I tell her that I stabbed a bloke a couple of months ago when he attacked me at the late-night burger wagon?

"I don't really know," I replied.

"Do you ever sit down and talk to your parents or anyone else?"

"No!"

"What do you think your main problems are?"

"I don't really know. I think maybe I drink too much."

"Why do you drink?"

"I just feel so nervous around people, I don't know what to say, or how to talk or make friends, I feel scared and alone, I don't feel like I belong, I am terrified that they are going to find out how alone and scared I feel. I am scared of being singled out and called names, I am scared they will find out that I can't read or write."

"Do you see any problems in the future for yourself?"

"My life seems to change dramatically every four or five years. I am terrified of being locked up, I need to be free." I felt this was not only true, but also a very good answer that may win some understanding and support from her.

"Do you feel that you need some help with your problems," she asked.

"I don't really know."

"OK, I am going to keep you here in the hospital until you go back to court. I will have you moved into the dormitory so you can watch TV if you want. I don't regard you as a risk to anyone. I am also going to give you a mild medication in order to help you relax a little. I will send a report to the court and see if we can help you. You will be glad to know that the police have decided not to proceed with a charge of attempted murder on them. Hopefully we will meet again and see what can be done to help you. If you go back out through the door one of the officers should be waiting for you."

The weeks pass. Tomorrow I go back to court. I am packed and ready to go, I can't stop thinking about it: what do they know about me, how will they see me, and what will become of me? I wish that it was all over and done.

I don't sleep very well, and I am up very early the next morning, eager to get the day over with. Six o'clock start, down to reception, deal with the paperwork, get my clothes back. Everyone's checking out everyone else by what clothes they wear, it's amusing what one can learn about people by the clothes they wear.

The wagon comes, I hate going in the wagon with its tiny little cells, looking out at the world through a tiny window as it passes by. I arrive at court just after 9am, I'm locked up in the cells in the basement until the court is ready; I walk up and down the cell trying to chill out, relax. 'Nothing to worry about, what will be will be, deal with it, it's only life, be a man,' I tell myself. 'But what about the injustice of it all, where is truth in this?' I ask. No love, no understanding of the reality of it. Where is the compassion? There is no compassion, no understanding: these people are only interested in the facts and the law; they live in a different world to me and they see things very differently, based on their own experience of their life. Upholding law and order at all costs is their priority. There is no place given for individual weakness or an inability to conform to their requirements. If someone finds it difficult to fit in, then they will be punished until they learn how to stay within the law.

I hear the keys in the cell door.

"Sims."

"Yea." I made a point of not saying 'sir'.

"Up you go, you know the way." I go up the stairs into the custody box. The courtroom is empty but for two people, an usher in a long black gown and a man in a suit at the centre desk, I think he's the court clerk, the one that runs everything, the one that makes sure that they all operate within the law.

Alfie won't be here today, I asked him not to come. I feel a little calmer now. 'It's not the end of the world, life will go on after today, it's all part of growing up and learning, life moves on,' I tell myself.

The courtroom is beginning to fill up. I wish I hadn't told

Alfie not to come, I would have liked to see his face, just for a while. Never mind.

"All stand," the man in the black gown shouts out.

Everyone stands; I stand. The three magistrates enter the courtroom from a door in the far corner, two men and one woman. The woman sits in the centre between the two men; she does most of the talking.

They check that they have got the right person:

"Stephan Sims, aged seventeen years, born on the fourth of July nineteen forty seven, is that you?" they ask. I get a bad feeling from them; they look very stern and make it clear that they are taking this matter extremely seriously. I feel like I have committed a murder.

The police did try to press for a charge of attempted murder. I can't believe it, how pathetic and sickening, the injustice of it! Two wrongs don't make a right, it just causes more bitterness and hate, and I find life tough enough. How can I show them an intelligent attitude if they are unable to show me one? I have little respect and regard for them, just as they have little for me. 'Just get on and do what you have already made your minds up to do, no need for all the formalities,' I think to myself, standing there looking back at them. They don't scare me, I hate them. If they knew what I was thinking and feeling inside they would have me locked up forever. God, I hate this world so much.

They talk amongst themselves for a while and then look back at me.

"We have considered your reports at length and agree that you are in need of correction. You will be sent to a borstal for a period of no less than six months and no more than twenty-four months. Stephan Sims you will be returned to Ashford Young Offenders Centre today and then onto Wormwood Scrubs for allocation to a suitable borstal for best training. We hope and trust that you will take full advantage of your training time away. Do you understand?"

Do I understand fuck! All I understand is that I won't be going home today, and for some time to come.

"Yeah," I answer back.

"The officer will take care of you now, please go down to the cell."

Down in the cells again, and a long wait for the wagon back to Ashford Young Offenders Centre. Well it's done now; there's no going back, what's done is done. I must try to learn from it, and yes I am scared and doubtful as to my future. I have no idea what to expect, I don't really know much about borstal and apparently each borstal is very different from the next.

Back to Ashford Young Offenders Remand Centre and all the red tape. Orders: 'do this', 'do that', 'don't speak', 'shut up and call me sir when I speak to you'. Sometimes I get scared that I'm going to say something that I'll regret like 'why don't you fuck off, you cunt!' That's what I really feel like saying. I bite my tongue and watch and learn in silence.

I will be glad to get back into my cell and into bed alone, just thinking. Sometimes I wish I could cry, but I can't. I can only feel sadness from somewhere deep inside. I wouldn't wish being me on anyone! I hate this so much – being moved around from place to place, different rooms, different cells, different courts, the transport wagons, the holding rooms, the noise, the constant talking of low life criminals, most of them scum! I hate them; they are so full of themselves, talking, talking about their crimes, boasting about how tough they are; jokes and stories.

I once had to listen to some black bloke boasting how he had to keep stabbing some old fellow in order to get his Rolex watch from him. I really wanted to say something to him, I almost did but I just stopped myself. 'Keep your mouth shut and say nothing,' I told myself.

There are four types of criminals in this place, as I see it: the broken pathetic no-hopers; the evil scumbags; the ones that try to look tough and talk tough; and the ones that are tough. And of course there are the screws to contend with – they are a completely different can of worms. I really don't know who's the worst – they deserve each other! The place is full of losers and I am one of them. But somehow I just don't seem to fit in. But what I do know is that I won't do much talking, I don't know how to and I have no desire to do so. I don't want to be here. What am I to trust in now? I must trust in my own ability to deal with all that will come to me, as it comes. I must show no fear, no emotions and be very careful whom I befriend.

They keep me at Ashford for three more weeks and then they move me out to Wormwood Scrubs, a real old prison in West London where they have a special wing just for borstal boys. This is called the allocation wing, where they do all the processing: age, type of crime committed, first time offenders, re-offenders, violent offenders, non-violent offenders, mentally ill, drug addicts, etc., etc. This place is more violent than Ashford, not so strict, not so controlled. We are allowed to interact and move around more and there are two or three hundred young boys, all full of themselves, waiting to go to borstal. There are many violent fights, mostly at mealtimes, about food or a wrong look.

I've had no contact with Janet, my girl friend, since I pushed her over the garden wall for stamping on the watch I bought her. She is just as crazy as I am, but strangely so. I got a letter from my mum, I don't think it was actually written by her, but she put her name to it. Probably written by one of my sisters, or maybe Alfie wrote it. Well at least she is trying to make some contact with me; I know she loves me really, but I am not sure how much I love her back. I feel a bit sorry for her – I have punished her so much. She means well, and she has changed over the past few years since I was first locked up. She is not really a heartless bitch; in fact I know she has a good heart. I remember when I was younger she said to me 'one day you will understand' and maybe now I am just beginning to get a glimpse of what she meant.

I have so much to think about when locked up in my cell. We are allowed to lie on our beds here and it makes life so much more bearable. Relaxing, feeling safe: locked in the cell no one can get to me; I'm free to think and listen to my thoughts. I think about my life over and over: how did I get myself into this mess, what's wrong with me? I think about all the crazy things I have done.

I have newspaper cuttings of Harry Roberts stuck on my wall; he shot dead three policemen last week. He's my hero, I love him to bits. What a hero, what a man! A real man with guts and courage to shoot down nasty policemen in the street, in broad daylight – that'll fucking make them think twice.

The screws made me take the news down from the cell wall. They asked me why I put it up, and I told them I put the news up to remind me how easy it is to lose one's way in life. How could I tell them the truth – what would you have done if you were me?

There is a lot of violence here. Yesterday at dinnertime some bloke got stabbed in the eye with a fork. They took him away to hospital with the fork still sticking out of his eye. He was screaming.

And last week a young boy committed suicide. I can't get him out of my mind. I remember looking at him, he was very shy and didn't speak much, he didn't know how – a bit like me. He was extremely vulnerable and, unlike me, was unable to protect himself when and if required.

I felt really sorry for him, I knew when I looked at him he was at risk. He shouldn't have been here. I wish I could have helped him in some way, looked after him, protected him from the vicious scum in here. I looked into his cell through the spy hole in the door: there was a big pile of blood on the floor stacked up just like cow shit, layer on top of layer, each layer becoming higher and smaller than the one below. I've never seen blood like that before. He's dead now; I have no Idea what he had done to be in here.

It made me think, and realise a few things: I knew then that I wanted to hurt my mother; that I wanted to challenge and hurt God in some way; that I wanted to punish and hurt myself. Crazy thoughts going through my mind, but vivid and clear – my intention was to hurt my mother as much as I possibly could even if it meant causing pain and suffering to myself! I am stuck in a crazy, dangerous, painful game of love and hate with her. I know she loves me deeply, but I won't let her love me. I will resist and destroy the very thing that I need and want the most.

I need to feel safe, I need to feel loved, I need to know that I belong. It seems that I have lost myself: I am becoming like two different people, one insensitive and the other oversensitive. I wish I knew what my problem was. Why do I have all these deep feelings of twisted defiance?

What will become of me? I will be eighteen tomorrow.

The Sound of Silent Words

If I am to travel this path set before me then I have much to learn.

I am able to see far beyond my understanding of it,
I am determined to search out life and test it until it breaks,
Or it breaks me.

I will search out God's true worth and intention for me,
I will make it painful and hard beyond reason,
I will find a way to punish my mother in order that I may love her,
I will make her feel my pain and my love.

I must find a way to test myself beyond compassion,
I will force their love for me,
If I am to know them, first I must know myself,
If I am to know myself I must learn the truth of my heart.

I will find a way to punish them,
This best be done by punishing myself,
Then we shall know the truth here.

I will punish and destroy all love that anyone may bring to me,
I will show them the truth of my integrity,
I will let nothing take away my pain,
I will never give it up,
Never.

My truth and my loyalty are to my own destruction if I am to fail,
And nothing less will I accept.

My lips are sealed and I will tell nothing more of this,
I will never submit to the greed and foolishness of this
world,
I spit on man's arrogance and vanity.
I will never surrender my truth and love,
I will be defiant beyond understanding.
I do not need to prove my love to anyone, least of all
God and myself.
God needs to prove himself to me!
And even I will learn how to submit before myself,
And bow down before all things.
If I fall, to cower and tremble at the sight of these words,
I am nothing but a fool.
Is there any choice for me in this? Yes!
I am shaken and feel concern for those around me,
I feel as if seen naked and bare,
Yet there is a boldness which is sure and unafraid in this.
I have no care, I seek only to survive unbroken from its
experience.
I have nothing to lose or gain for it is already done, of this
I feel sure.
So what is my part in it, and why am I to cry for others
unable to see?
I am done, and do only what needs to be done
For there is a long way to go yet.

Chapter 12

I feel like a sheep in wolf's clothing, that's how it is for me. Every time the cell door is unlocked I need to put on my suit of deception, which comes with a warning: 'think twice if you have any intention of hostile exploitation or dominance'. I may have nothing to say, but things are never quite what they seem. There is an emptiness about me, unsure as to the potential outcome, probably dangerous – and very scared. You know what they say about trapped wounded animals.

Every day they let us out into the exercise yard where we walk around in circles, in groups of twos and threes. A few walk alone, myself one of them, a long walk of isolation to be seen by all. How do they see me: strong or weak? Do I think that I am better than them? Don't I need them? Don't I need to be with them? Why am I walking alone? It's so agonising and painful, I find it so difficult to do, it's almost unbearable.

I try to think it through logically, but the outcome is always the same. I feel like a sheep among hungry lions all around me – I stink of fear. It's just a matter of time before I am found out and then they will tear me apart. In a moment of terror, I can't help ask myself, 'what is it that I am really so scared of?' I feel naked, unclothed, seen by all. They will single me out, laugh and mock me. I stand alone, not belonging, hated and despised, full of fear. They will beat me to death, I will not be able to defend myself. I don't want them to hate me, I want to feel safe, I want to feel that I belong. Why do I always have to be so alone and full of fear? It's the same old problem, it never goes away.

There is something else that bothers me, something much deeper and much more terrifying, but I just can't see it, can't grasp it. It hides itself away, terrified, deep down in my soul. I feel sick with emotion. It's the same as the school in the playground, only ten times worse. For these guys are vicious predators, hungry for helpless victims to prey on: the strongest and the most ruthless will claim the day in here. I feel overwhelmed; I can't match these guys. They are fast and loud, they know how to talk, boast and tell stories; they tell jokes and laugh amongst themselves; strength in numbers is the name of the game – a good strategy. They are tough and hard, and they give little time or consideration for any weakness shown. I have little to offer them: I don't know a single joke and even if I did I would be too shy to tell it; I don't tell stories and I seldom find anything to laugh about. The quiet timid boy that took his life, I understand very well why, but it's not for me. I need to find another away to deal with my fears and problems walking out in the exercise yard. I need to keep myself alive and deal with my terrifying aloneness.

I lay on my bed thinking of home, thinking of the two boys from where I live, the ones that were hung. One of them was only eighteen. I think of all the eighteen-year-olds that were sent to war, and never came home. Eighteen years old, so young to die, dropped down through the floor and hung by your neck, snapping your vertebrae apart and crushing your wind pipe, leaving you choking until dead. What would be going through your mind just before you died?

I feel a cold chill enter my cell, I feel scared and very alone. Did those boys have any idea what they were doing? I don't suppose they cared at the time, but surely they didn't intend to kill. Why should I care about it, people do what they do, what should it matter to me? From my bedroom at home I had watched Harris go in and out of the front door just across the street, I had seen his desperate, lonely and sad mother begging for compassion. A mother's love for a son is compelling, I felt her hopeless pain and it somehow locked itself into me. But what about the boy they killed – where is my pity for him and his mother? Maybe I need to see things from the other side: four of them beat the boy to death – what was it like for him and his family? He had planned to get married, his family must have been devastated. He was just a young man, a boy – what did he know about life? Did he ask for mercy? Was he shown any compassion?

I wonder where is my part in this and what the difference is between them and me. Why do I carry a knife when I go out? Why did I stab that bloke at the hot-dog wagon? I could have killed him; his family would have been broken, and suffered a lifetime of grief and loss just because of my fears and insecurity about people and the world. What about all the other things I've done that I haven't told you about? I can dwell in the past and wallow in the self-pity of my mistakes, or is now the time to look at the truth of who and what I really am?

I am trying desperately to find my way in life, trying to grow up and become a man, and find a way to belong in the world, and find what I am here for. The reality is that I am locked up and waiting to go to borstal, six months to two years the judge said. Two years, that's a long time; six months, that's not so bad – I've almost done three already counting my time on remand. How do they decide how long a person must stay? I find that a little worrying.

Why did I get so drunk, why did I steal the car? If only the owner hadn't have left the keys in the ignition! Yes, I stole a nice shiny Jaguar car, which rammed into a police car, and then I assaulted the policemen. The charge of attempted murder was dropped. Yes, OK, it was wrong, I shouldn't have done it; I know I could have killed someone and then I would have been in real big trouble.

I keep getting into fights with the police – why won't they just leave me alone? They always seem to want to confront me for some reason and I find it very difficult to back down. I don't know why I need to get drunk every day, I haven't got a clue – maybe I have a drink problem. Am I really so wild and unruly? I just seem to hurt so much from somewhere inside, and I don't know what to do with it. They say I am highly strung – whatever that means.

I don't know how to talk and make friends, not sure that I even want to talk and make friends. I don't read or write, don't really know how, don't know the alphabet, can't say my times tables (other than ten times or two times and also five times tables – those I do know!) How did I manage to stay at college for so long? What a nightmare that was, but I did do very well at the practical side of carpentry, in fact I really enjoyed it. If only I could have found a way to stay and learn how to read and write. Maybe I should have told someone of my problems. I didn't have a problem working on the fruit and veg stall in the high street. I've got no problem when it comes to dealing with money matters. I can play two board games: drafts and chess. I really enjoy a game of chess, that's one thing I did learn at school, in the drama class it was. I've never read a book and it's difficult for me to write a letter. One of the other boys here did help me write a letter home last week, but I don't like to ask!

The days are very long, with very little to do to pass the time. What do I do? I look and study my cell, I study my mind and thoughts, and many times I send my mind outside the walls of the prison to see what's going on in the world, and then back home to see my family. I wish someone could help me. Maybe the doctor I saw at Ashford will help me – Dr Ellis her name was.

I think of Alfie my stepdad, a Jew from Germany, with an English father and a Jewish mother, at the age of eighteen he was serving in the Royal Navy fighting the Germans in the war – a strange pedigree. And my mother, a violent bitch and a whore, who I find difficult to love. And me: an unwanted bastard child of a evil Nazi German bomber pilot – an even stranger pedigree – true, false or just stories? I have four half-sisters; I find it difficult to understand the meaning of a half-sister, either they are my sisters or they're not. And what other secrets do I hold? I carry the shame of causing the death of my dear friend from my childhood days. I have deep feelings of not belonging, and fears of being found out. I have no qualifications and no job, no trade or skills to offer. I often find myself in conflict with aggressive loud people, with or without the consumption of alcohol. I am labelled a hard street-fighter capable of vicious rage, with a criminal record for violence on police officers. I was kicked out of college and denied access in to the Army.

The irony is that I see myself as the good guy, the hero, standing up for justice and good, for the downtrodden underdogs. I fail to see that I have done wrong to anyone. I would not wish the feelings I carry on any person – ten minutes in my head and you would be broken and screaming to get out.

I constantly look for the true value of myself and my existence here. Searching for understanding, I study the screws and their daily routine. I try to look into the other inmates, looking for signs of what was really going on with them, but it's not so easy, they are quick to look away. Back in my cell I think of my family, Alfie and my uncle Jack; thinking of them gives me hope and strength, helps me believe in myself.

I receive a letter from my youngest sister. She writes of chasing after butterflies: 'The more you chase after something,' she says, 'the less chance you may have of catching it'. She writes on about being still and waiting awhile. 'Sometimes it may just come to you and settle on you,' she tells me, and at that very moment I see up at my window a butterfly! What kind of magic is this? I am deeply moved as I look up – dancing in the sunlight, a yellow butterfly. I watch intently, as if seeing for the first time. I slowly move to my chair, placing it near to the window, remembering my sister's words about being still and not so quick to chase after. I stand up on the chair which brings my eyes level with the window sill; slowly I move my hand out onto the stonework, and wait motionless with expectation and trust in my sister's words. The butterfly hops around in the sunlight, then it flutters over and settles on my arm. This moment I shall never forget. It filled me with a wonderful feeling – a feeling of love.

How could I ever know the truth of that single moment? 'Sometimes if one is still and quiet it will just come and settle upon you.' Does this apply to all things in life, I ask myself. I remember then, in that moment, that I was different, that I had a purpose that I could never let go of. I can't give up my mission in this lifetime for any amount of money, love, feelings of safety or belonging; no matter how difficult or painful – the sorrow and grief of the suffering and feelings of my loneliness – I am set on a path of learning and hardship which I cannot deny or forget. I must find a way to embrace my purpose and trust in it. There seems no escape for me. But how will I survive this? Something deep down in my soul cries so! A terrible, sorrowful pain that constantly weeps for the human race, men crying in war, for the terrible wrongs done. I see too many things and so vivid.

I am so fearful of what life holds for me. My problem with reading and writing has a big effect on me. It's not easy trying to hide my torturing disability: even when I am asleep it chases after me, terrible dreams, nightmares so disturbing. The feelings it brings make me want to be sick, strike me dumb, I am unable to talk. Just like at school in the playground, struck dumb, unable to move. And now it's the same in the prison yard, but I just keep walking, praying that I go unnoticed – little chance of that!

I tell no one of my problem, but I must find a way to avoid the exercise yard. When the screws unlock for exercise they leave the cell door open, the inmates come out and slam the cell door behind them when leaving for the yard. The screws come around for the second time, checking the cells are empty, looking in through the spy hole, and sometimes even opening the door and looking inside. Sometimes they look under the bed before slamming shut the cell door. I have worked out a way of staying in my cell: I have made up a support strap that will hold me up off the floor, keeping my hips up tight to the underside of my bed. I will try it out tomorrow!

I think about it overnight. What will I say if I get caught? I can't really see any problems, they will only find me if they look under the bed. Why would they want to look under the bed? Only if they were down on their numbers, someone missing. They count the head numbers out and they count the head numbers in, lock in all the inmates and do a final count at the same time, if the numbers add up no one's missing and there are no problems.

I tried it out and all went to plan, no problems, so now I can do as I wish, I am free to choose the solitude of my own company or the freedom of walking out in the prison yard in the sunlight and fresh air, alone or not. It seems to make a difference to my state of mind and I get a buzz from working against the system. It empowers me and makes me feel a little different, but this time in a positive sense.

I always keep my cell clean and tidy and I have a book now, which I intend to read to the best of my ability. The book's title is Treaka (I am sure I've spelt it wrong). Anyway, I think it's based on a true story of a young man eager to sail around the world in his small sailing boat with a cat that sometimes goes mad and runs up and down the mast. That doesn't surprise me – what else would a cat do on a sailing boat?

I get enough money each week to buy a half ounce of smoking tobacco, one packet of Rizla rolling papers and a box of matches, which lasts me just about the week until next payday. Soap, shampoo and toothpaste are a rarity in here: I use salt to clean my teeth and prison soap to wash my hair when I get the chance. I've now learnt how to split one matchstick into four useable sticks. Some of the boys make candles and some boys use a lighter flint to set aflame a Rizla paper, quite ingenious. The usual method for moving things around during lock-up time is a length of mailbag sewing thread, about ten to fifteen yards, tied onto a prison boot-polish tin. Adjusting the length of the line out of the window gives enough movement for exchanges between twelve cells on four levels. The tin is lowered down and then swung left and right, and after the exchange the tin is pulled back up. But you need to be on good terms with the other cellmates. I always make sure that I don't need to, I am dependant only on myself and my own ability, though I am always ready and eager to learn from others. I often wonder how the other boys pass the time of day in their cells alone.

The food is OK though there never seems to be enough, but at least it comes three times a day. My cell is about the same size as my little bedroom at home, the only difference being the window and no wardrobe to hang clothes – you don't need a wardrobe in here, the only clothes you get are what you wear.

The weeks pass by slowly and I am looking forward to getting out of here soon into a borstal, I am still waiting to be allocated. The doctor I saw at Ashford Young Offenders Remand Centre has contacted me and will be coming to see me here next week. What will I tell her? I am eighteen years old and waiting to go to borstal, and my only ambition is to be a cop killer. I'd better not tell her that! What did I tell her last time, can't remember now. Shall I tell her that as a child no one ever told me what to do or how to be, what to say, how to say it? That no one told me what was right or wrong, no one told me when to go to bed, when to get up, when to go to school, what to eat, when to eat, who to play with, who not to play with, how to play, how to talk, how to make friends, what to wear? No one ever told me anything; I had to find out for myself. Thank God for my nan and Mrs B.

   I lay on my bed thinking of the past and all the things I've done, trying to make sense of it. What am I to tell her – shall I tell her what it's really like to be me? Maybe I will tell her my life story, if she has the time. Maybe I will tell her that I am the unwanted bastard child of an evil German Nazi bomber pilot who killed the parents of my best and only friends. Maybe I will tell her that I hate my mother and sometimes I have feelings that I would like to kill her. Maybe I will tell her that my mother is a whore and when I was a child I would often blackmail her.

Maybe I will tell her that I killed her cat and my uncle's canary – and my friend Carl. Maybe I will tell her that I remember coming from a place somewhere before I was born and that sometimes I float out of my body. Maybe I will tell her that my angel comes to me in times of extreme sadness and times of danger, about my grandmother dying when I was four years old and about Mrs B who took me into her home for safety and then died, leaving me alone again. I could tell her about all the bad things I have done. I could tell her of my childhood dream of becoming a racing jockey. I could tell her that I am scared shitless, terrified of people – human beings – and I have no desire to be on the planet.

The meeting comes and I tell her none of these things. It was a short meeting, just twenty minutes; she told me that she had done all that she could to get me into her borstal, and all was now final and agreed: Feltham borstal in West London, not far from my family home. I will be moving out in two weeks.

"I am going to see what can be done to help you," she tells me.

Sounds promising, I thought to myself.

I go back to my cell and lie on my bed, thinking and questioning as always. What have I learnt here? What will it be like at the borstal? Will she be able to help me? Will I be safe there? I must find a way to change, I must find away to express myself without violence. I need to find a way to communicate. I really want to make things easier for myself. I am looking forward to making a new start.

Chapter 13

Two weeks pass soon enough and I am off in the prison wagon to Feltham borstal, West London; from what I can tell there are nine or ten other boys also going to the same borstal. We go through the same process on arrival and then we are split into four groups, each going to a different location. There are four accommodation blocks: north, south, east, and west; myself and two other lads will be going to East House, each block holds forty to fifty boys. The two lads with me have little to say and we share the same anxiety. As we enter the block the tension grows and all eyes are upon us, looking for weakness or dangers; in that stressful moment we huddle together like sheep.

We are constantly assessed, watched by the borstal staff and the other boys for attitude. One of the boys that I came in with was put in the serving kitchen to give out food at meal times; this was always considered to be a privileged position, especially for a new arrival. He quickly became dominant and aggressive when dishing out the food; I think it must have been too much for him – it can be extremely difficult trying to suppress your fear and feelings of vulnerability. Some hours later he staggered out of the toilets with blood streaming from his nose, he was sent to the hospital for treatment, on his return he was attacked again, this time a metal teapot was smashed into his face. The bone in his nose was pushed up into his head; he was rushed to hospital for an emergency operation and blood transfusion. He almost died.

I realised then that you needed to be very careful who you spoke to and in what manner and attitude you spoke. It was early days and there was much learning to be done; I was good at keeping my mouth shut and looking and studying what was really going on and what the dangers were, who the daddies were – a daddy was the name given to the boy most feared, the hardest or toughest, the ones that ran things, telling the other boys what they can do or, in most cases, what they can't do. Be sure to know who is dangerous, who is stupid, who to avoid, and who to show respect to. Best keep myself to myself and deal with situations as they come, stay cool and calm, there are many days to go.

The gym is a good place to see who is really tough and who isn't. There were many different levels going on in this place, mostly unseen, and you have to be very careful not to make too many mistakes or to make enemies. There was a pecking order: newcomers were on the bottom run of the ladder, you were nobody, just do as you are told; it takes time to work your way up. For me the gym was the best place to be – no talking and lots of hard work. I felt safe there, this is where I could shine and get myself some credibility. It was scary and extremely painful, but somehow I found a way to feed on it and enjoy it, I felt empowered every time we went there, which was every day to begin with.

One day the PT instructor divided us up: the boys with tattoos on one side and the boys without tattoos on the other side. He made us hang from the wall bar on each side of the gym and look into each other's eyes. "Don't be intimidated by a bit of paint," he said, "People use tattoos to make themselves look tough because they are scared. Remember that we are all the same in here. Keep your mouth shut and work hard and you won't fall out with me."

There were about twelve of us and I am sure he felt confident that he could take care of himself, having no fear of us. I thought it was a good speech, me being one of the boys with tattoos.

When not in the gym we would be put to work doing some kind of cleaning job, scrubbing long stone floors, corridors, or polishing hard lino floors – the floors were so durable I thought they'll last longer than the brickwork! I remember one day when I was scrubbing I was having a really bad feeling, hostile and crazy – maybe I needed a drink or something – there was an officer walking up and down really close to me and I kept getting these really scary, crazy thoughts of hitting him over the head and taking his keys to escape out of there. It was really touch and go, at one point I come very near to doing it, but then I thought, could I hit him hard enough to knock him out cold, or would I hit him too hard and kill him? I am so glad I decided against it, for a moment it really did scare me.

Sometimes I wonder if I am just not right in the head, I just feel like a wild animal caged up, my only desire is to get free, I see the officers as aggressors, wicked and evil with no love or concern for me. Some of them are real bullies, spiteful, and nasty like little boys in the school playground. I am sure most of them were bullied at school or even by their parents. I grew up thinking that adults knew everything, including how I was feeling; that they would do the right thing. It was some time before I found out that actually they knew little more than I did, and had little concern for me or any of the other boys.

I was beginning to feel more confident now as the days passed and I settled in and started to make a few friends – friendships that were formed in the gym. Jeff was a real straight and genuine guy, decent and seemingly honest with self-respect and consideration for others, I never did ask him what he was in for. George was a bit of a tough ruffian with little concern for anyone else, but he never made things difficult for anyone and kept himself to himself. George and Jeff seemed to really like me, and we formed a strong bond. Unfortunately for me Jeff was sent to a different borstal some weeks later, an open borstal. He seemed happy to go, I think that the borstal was nearer to his home and I was pleased for him. I still think of him and wonder how he is doing in his life.

George and I decided to give up smoking and set up a little tobacco business. Tobacco barons they were called in there. It's totally against the rules and looked down on, as it is a form of controlling other inmates. You loan out tobacco one week and get back twice as much next week – or money, food, sugar, clothes, basically anything you want – a bit like moneylenders on the outside. It made life much easier, but it came with high risks – risks that I wasn't really aware of. I think George had done it before, he seemed to know what he was doing; as for me, I just wanted to give up smoking and it seemed like a good idea to have more than everyone else. If the other blokes were weak and desperate enough to get themselves in debt just for a small amount of tobacco then that was their stupid problem! But sometimes it wasn't so easy to get back what you were owed, some arrangement would need to be made, but no one ever got hurt in the process, not to my knowledge.

I soon found that no one could be trusted in there. Things had been going very well, but then George got pulled in; he was more open about his dealings than I was. They took him off to the block for interrogation, and it wasn't long before they moved him out to a place called Reading. Reading was a very notorious extreme punishment centre for boys, where they broke the hardest of young criminals. I had heard really terrible stories about this place; my biggest fear was that I would be sent there. I would never have seen home again if I had, I just wouldn't be able to deal with that level of abuse and injustice without a violent response. There were stories of beatings, and many suicides – poor old George. But I was sure that he would deal with it, adapting to the daily routine of being screamed and shouted at. They pulled me in next, down the block for interrogation. They kept me there for three days; they took all my belongings, searching for evidence. Fortunately I didn't have any more than my weekly earnings would allow.

I was really worried that they would send me off to join George. I refused to say or admit to anything – that was easy for me, it was in my nature to be defiant and say nothing, and I didn't like to speak much anyway. They said that George had told them everything and that I was also involved in the dealings of lending out tobacco. 'Not true', I said, and that's all I was prepared to say. I was well aware of the way they worked when interrogating: they would say that your mate or mates had told them everything so you'd just as well confess, and denying it would do you no good.

Three days later I was taken back to East House Block with no charges and no punishment; George had told them nothing of my involvement. God, did I feel lucky! It was a big shake up for me; Reading was the last place I needed to be. Now I sat eating alone at my table – no Jeff and no George. I'd best keep my head down and stick to working hard.

I had been given a place working in the carpenter's shop as an apprentice joiner, second year practical and theory. I was over the moon about it – I think Dr Ellis, the psychiatrist, may have had something to do with it. I know Alfie will be pleased, I'll write and tell him.

I really enjoyed working in the carpenter's workshop; I have my own workbench and my own set of tools, which I sign in and out at the beginning and end of each day. We also do two or three evenings a week in the classroom, away from the stress and madness of the other boys. Things are starting to look good for me now, I am settled in, lucky not to have been sent to Reading and now Dr Ellis is seeing me every week. She is OK, we get along all right, but sometimes we sit there in silence for long periods and I don't understand why. I wish she would help me talk about things: by the time I am ready to open up it's time to go back to the main block.

But my world falls apart yet again, and so quickly. I was working in the carpenter's workshop putting a new window frame together. One of the joints was too tight. I should have taken it apart and eased off one side with a chisel and then it would have fitted together very easily, but I decided to take a wooden mallet and use force. The training officer saw me and went ballistic, he came rushing at me, screaming and shouting. My arm raised up with the mallet in my hand, I turned to him and said, "Fuck off or I will smash your fucking head in!"

Off to the punishment block again, I get nine days locked up in solitary and three days on bread and water, loss of all wages and privileges. The worst of it was that I was kicked off the course, just like when I was sixteen at college, same problem. Alfie will be disappointed with me. I wish people would just leave me alone.

I really like it in solitary. PT twice a day – I love it, I feed on it. The PTI likes me, he shows me respect; I don't have to speak to anyone; solitude, peace and quiet, time to think; no stress, no fear, no violence and my own space.
Dr Ellis came to see me.
"Why don't you try writing things down?"
She orders one of the officers to make sure that I have a writing book and a pencil, that's the only thing that I am allowed to have in the cell other than the Bible, which I sometimes try to read but make little sense of.

For the first time in my life I start to write. I must try to find a way to communicate without violence. I can't stop writing – maybe sixty per cent of it is unreadable or spelt wrong, but I am writing! Eighteen years old and I am going to start writing my life story for Dr Ellis. She reads my stuff every week. And I also start going to AA meetings once a week, the guy comes in and reads and talks to us, a real nice guy, he tells us that he won't tell a lie for fear of going back on the drink. The inmates that come to the meetings are somehow different to the other boys; they tend to be more honest. I get friendly with one of them, he's twenty years old, a real nice fellow, but he just won't take any shit from anyone, least of all the borstal officers. He's married with two children. His wife has gone off with someone else and he's going a bit crazy over it, understandably so. He ends up down the punishment block, smashes up the wall clock and one of the telephones. He got sectioned and sent to Broadmoor, a mental institution. It scared me, I didn't realize it was so easy to get sectioned – I had better look out for myself. But some days the boredom takes over.

I've got two new friends now, Taffy from Cardiff and Smithy from the East End of London, always looking for trouble. One day Taffy and I took hold of one the lads – the lad was a little simple, easy game. We lifted him up off the floor and hung him over the balcony by his ankles. He was screaming, terrified, and we were laughing as his ankles began to slip through our sweating grip on him. We could have lost him, but this all added to the excitement and the rush of adrenaline. We just managed to pull him back. If we had dropped him he would have not survived the fall down to the concrete floor below. We laughed about it for weeks and somehow after that day we took a liking to the boy, Toby his name was. We never bothered him again and in a weird way we even felt some respect and responsibility for him.

We talk about barricading ourselves into the games room just for a laugh, something to break the boredom. I feel at a loss after losing my job in the carpenter's workshop, I'd lost my chance of sitting the City & Guilds papers and getting qualified. I go and study the lay out in the games room: there's a piano, a ping-pong table, a small sofa, tables and chairs. I work it out: put out end to end, all the furniture will fit between the far wall and the heavy door, the only way in and out.

I go and tell Taffy and Smithy. They have changed their minds.

"Let's do it tomorrow," Smithy said.

"Fuck you, I am going to do it now!"

I was so excited about how easy it was going to be, I wanted to vent my anger about being kicked out of the carpenter's shop. I rushed into the games room, telling the other boys to get out if they didn't want to be locked in. They don't take much notice of me, so I slammed the door shut and started rearranging the piano and furniture. It all fit together very nicely; the lads thought it was a big joke and carried on playing their board games. One of the boys was supposed to be some kind of sex offender as the rumours had it, but I had no idea what he was in for, he just looked like he may be dodgy.

"You're staying here," I said. I knocked him to the floor and started strangling him. He stopped breathing. I didn't expect him to stop breathing so easily; I thought that I had killed him. Maybe he was in shock – fuck, I've got to do something to make him breath again! Mouth to mouth on this shit-bag, I had to do something: I pinched his nose and gave one big hard blow down his throat, and to my relief he started breathing again. There wasn't a sound in the room, everyone was quiet now and knew that I meant business. The screws turned up with Kangos and started knocking a hole through the wall. I told the lads to remove the tables and piano, which they quickly did. Down the block again – six days solitary, three days bread and water.

They let me out of the punishment block and I went back to work, moving stuff around the borstal. I had to work with a really nasty screw, nasty and horrible. I saw him stamp on a tiny mouse one day and he was so full of himself about it, really proud he was; he was a short man with a very big nose and an even bigger ego. I hated him, and I don't think he was very fond of me. One day he started poking me in my chest with his index finger telling me that I was just a number, just a borstal boy.

"Don't fucking touch me!" I screamed right into his horrible face, and then hit it. He had his whistle in his mouth and was just about to blow it when I struck him hard and fast. He fell down cold to the floor, I wanted to stamp on his head, but I stopped myself.

"You fucking bastard, you're lucky I don't kill you!" I screamed at him. What the fuck will I do now, shall I take his keys and make a run for it?

I walked down to the punishment block and banged on the door,

"I need to come in," I said, I've just knocked out one of the officers."

I was in big trouble now. A visiting court was set up to come to the borstal. I had to go and stand before them; they would decide my fate. Reports were made up from just about everyone in the borstal that knew me.

"We have read your reports and we have decided to give you one last chance. Dr Ellis has spoken up for you and wants you to be moved to the hospital wing under her care and supervision. We have agreed to this, but be warned: this is your very last chance, any more trouble and you will get the rubber stamp. Do you know what the rubber stamp is?"

"No," I replied.

"You will be sectioned and sent to Broadmoor Mental Institution indefinitely. You must remain in solitary for the time being, and you will receive a punishment of nine days bread and water. Do you understand?"

"Yes," I replied, and off I went back to the punishment block. I couldn't believe it, no extra time – the borstal officers were not happy about it.

I was quick to learn how to use my mind: it's a very long day locked in your cell for 24 hours with nothing to do, just waiting for your bread and water to come. Normally boys would go for the crustless bread, but I chose to go for the crusted bread-ends. They were harder and allowed me to chew on the bread and make it last much longer. In the process I would close my eyes and visualise a large lump of steak cooking in a frying pan. I could see it, I could hear the sizzling as it cooked, and I could also smell it. With my eyes closed I would take a large bite at the crusty bread, chew on it hard and long. It felt and tasted just like steak and it was absolutely delicious – I enjoyed every moment of it. Even though my body was locked up, my mind was free to roam and create its own reality. It was a wonderful experience, learning how to be truly free.

Chapter 14

Monday morning comes and it's a new day. I look out through the window of the hospital block and see a big black limo, just like Carl's limo parked outside his house all those years ago, a hearse, and a coffin in the back, a body inside, one of the boys committed suicide. Where would I rather be right now: in that coffin, or in my body, alive, right here and now, with all my emotions and feeling? I realise then how precious life is. When you are dead, you are dead for a very long time. I don't want to be dead, I want to be alive, and I am going to stay alive for as long as I can no matter how much it hurts!

I meet with Dr Ellis again.

"Do you think you're ready to go back to work yet?" she asks. I make no reply.

"Well I think we need to get you back to work. I am going to put an application in for you to work outside, in and around the borstal, doing repair, maintenance and carpentry work with a good friend of mine, Mr Bennett. He is a really nice man I am sure you will get on with him. How does that sound?"

"Sounds good to me."

"How long have you been here now?"

"Just coming up for one year," I reply.

"Good, so you should be coming up for a home-leave period of five days soon. Will you come back if we let you home for five days?" I made no reply. "I think you need to be working and doing something you're good at, something that you enjoy. What do you think?"

"Yes I would really like to be doing something with my life, I would really like to be able to read, write, and spell."

"I know you would. Let's get you working with Mr Bennett, and see if we can get you some home leave. Let's see how that goes."

I tell her that I am really grateful for her understanding and support.

I have been working with Mr Bennett for six weeks now and we get on very well. He takes the time to teach me things and allows me to get on with the job. He is very calm when he prepares and plans out how best to go about completing the work. I watch him and see how he studies and assesses the job, first making notes as to what materials are needed, size and quantities, and what tools are needed. He gets it all set up and planned out, and then we start work. He always tells me what he wants me to do and lets me get on with it until I come up against a problem. Then we look at how the problem can be solved. Things are looking good and I am feeling positive in myself.

I have been given notice of my home leave date, three weeks time. I am excited about it but I feel a little nervous. I don't know what I'm scared about. This place feels like home now: I feel safe here, I just need to work and stay out of trouble, keep away from conflict, bad vibes, and nasty people. How I love to learn how to do things.

The days seem to pass quickly and in no time it's the date of my release. Five days home leave, but I must come back – a daunting thought! God, that must be difficult: to turn around and walk back in of your own free will. I feel a little uncertain, not really knowing what to expect or how I will feel about things back home in my little room, what will I do for five days. Alfie, my mum, and my four sisters, I don't even know how to have a conversation with them, what will I say to them?

I arrive home having no idea how I got there. I go up to my old room, newly painted, and a comfortable soft bed. I lie down on the bed, gazing out through the window up into the blue sky. I am nineteen years old now – I am not sure if that's old or young, I feel almost a man. It feels good to be back home in my own room. I feel safe and sure of myself.

My mother has changed. I feel sorry for her and I'm secretly ashamed for the way I have treated her over the years. Alfie is working as always, he tells me that he has got me a job as a carpenter, with a friend of his from the orphanage he was left in when he was a child. The job involves travelling around the country, assembling timber portable buildings, the same buildings I used to make as an apprentice joiner when I was sixteen.

My uncle Jack has been asking about me; he wants to meet up. My mum's fixed me up with a date with one of the local girls. I am a bit overwhelmed by it all, maybe I've done her an injustice. I need to find a way to be a good son and a good brother.

The house is much cleaner than I remember it being, new carpet, TV, a radiogram, three-piece suite, and everyone seems to be happy. I am looking forward to starting a new life for myself.

I take an early night. I go up and lay on my bed thinking, trying to take it all in. What happened to me over the last three years? Life is so strange. I am home in my own room, free from fear and anxiety, four sisters that seem to love and care about me.

I am nineteen years old, just setting out in life. I have no idea what life holds for me, but I am hopeful. First I need to get myself back to borstal and complete three more months, and then it is a new life for me. No holding me back, the world is mine; I have a life to get on with. I need to be somebody, I need to justify my life and find a purpose. I need to learn how to read and write. That's what I need to do! I need to learn to read and write.

Going back was hard, I just couldn't get my head to understand what it was that I was required to do, go back inside for three more months. Going back felt really strange, everything seemed dream-like. I think someone took me back by car and dropped me off at the car park; I walked in on my own. I remember walking up to the main doors and requesting they let me in – that felt really weird. The doors opened and they let me in, then they unlocked the second steel door that allows entry into the main block, and then into East House, knocking, banging at the door again to get in. Strip off, give up all your clothes and possessions, get searched and then back into your borstal clothes again – what a roller coaster of emotions – and walking out through another locked door into the dining room where all the lads were assembled for the meal. Checking out faces for changes and old mates. It's only been five days but it feels like a lifetime. It's very confusing and extremely stressful.

I couldn't sleep to start with, then after a couple of days I got settled in again. Three more months – twelve weeks. How long will it take to pass? Will I manage to complete it? Will I stay out of trouble, stay calm, not get involved in dodgy dealings, stay clean, not give anyone any reason to want to fight me? Just do one day at a time and it will soon pass.

Dr Ellis got me back into night classes, carpentry and joinery theory. I still hung around with Taffy and Smithy. The days seemed to go slowly. I tried to get into my work with Mr Bennett; I did enjoy it and I was learning, but sometimes the days were long and boring. I couldn't wait to get out and back home, out of there. The girl my mum fixed me up with wrote to me, she had her own flat and she said that I could move in with her if I wanted to when I am ready. Sounds good to me.

I've got a release date now, 19/9/67. Good news, but my world was about to fall apart again. One night when going to joinery study class myself and one other boy were passing the punishment block and the door opened. One of the screws came out and spoke to the other boy.

"You, take these trays back to the kitchen," he ordered, four metal dinner trays, the same ones used as weapons at Ashford Remand some years earlier. The boy with me went to pick them up. I spoke up, I don't know why or what got into me.

"That's not his job," I said, "We are going to classes at the carpenter's workshop. Don't do it."

"OK Sims, you take them back."

"No," I said.

"OK, off you go to your class."

On the way back they were waiting for me, two of them outside the block.

"Sims, in you go. We need to talk to you." It felt serious, slow, direct and planned. What the hell was going on?

They put me in a cell and left me there for two hours before they returned.

"You'll be staying here for the night. Get your bedding in and make your bed up, you'll be seeing the governor in the morning."

It was a long night. Why did I open my mouth? It was nothing to do with me! I was sure things would turn out OK. The morning came and I was put before the governor, we had met many times before. He had only one eye. Sometimes Taffy and Smithy would make a joke about him to me. "Hey Steve, who's this?" they would say, sitting on a chair pretending to drive with one eye shut, rocking from side to side as if the car had run over something. "The story goes that he had run over and killed one of his children," they would laugh every time. I couldn't help wondering if he had ever seen us mocking his misfortune and loss.

I stood up in front of him, gave my name and number.

"You are charged with disobeying an order given by one of the borstal officers. Is this correct?" I stood there just staring into his eyes.

"Well, is it correct or not?"

"Yes sir," I replied.

"How long have you been here now?" he asked, looking at my reports and records, "I see you have just returned from home leave."

"Yes sir."

"I don't think you will be ready for the outside world for a while yet, do you?"

I made no reply.

"If you were given the chance to take the trays back would you take them back?" I thought about it for a while, I best be smart and humble myself I thought.

"If I was given the chance I would take them back, sir."

"OK, you will be returned to the cells for three days with a loss of privileges for nine days and an order for you to serve an extension of three more months onto your sentence, meaning that your release date will be deferred by three months. You may go back to the cell."

"OK Sims, this way, the governor's finished with you now." I came so close to calling the governor a cunt.

I'm back in my cell, thinking hard, devastated by my situation. Why, why is life so hard on me? Why can't I get it right? Deep, dark thoughts came into my mind. I returned to the main block a very different person, something had changed in me. All that had gone before was of no relevance now. I had lost sight of ever returning home or being a normal person, free from depression and fear. I would never find a way to belong in this world.

I spoke with Taffy and Smithy about breaking out. They seemed up for it, but I had visions of much more: I wanted to go to the local gun shop just off the main high street in my home town; I had been there several times, I knew where the ammunition was kept. I spoke of robbing the shop and then going back to the borstal with a gun; I wanted to chase and kill two or three officers, that was my real intention. I think it scared Taffy and Smithy, they kept coming up with reasons and excuses not to do it.

"Let's think about it," they said, "maybe next week."

I decided to go alone, I had a good knowledge now of how the borstal was laid out: four main blocks, North, South, East, and West, with the kitchen and laundry at the centre; all the workshops were to the south east, the hospital block was south west, all the admin offices were located in the block to the north east and the punishment block and never-used swimming pool were to the north west. One way in and one way out, a car park with a visiting block nearby on the far east side, and a nine-foot brick wall with an arch top running all the way round, leaving only one opening manned with a barrier to let cars in and out.

I made two lengths of wood that fitted together, easily carried and concealed. When put together at an angle they would give me a step up of eighteen inches against the wall. The wall was nine feet high, less eighteen inches leaves seven feet six inches. I was sure that I would be able to reach up to the top and pull myself over; I was fit and strong. The red-band trustee always collected me from Mr Bennett after a day's work to take me back to the main block just before teatime. He turned up on time as usual. On the way I told him I was going to make a run for it.

"Just in case anyone is watching I am going to slap your face. I want you to fall down on the ground and stay there for about ten minutes before you sound the alarm." He was a sensible boy and was due for release. I slapped him hard hoping to make a mark to his face so it was clear that he had been attacked. He fell to the ground and I was off in a flash.

My heart had never pounded so hard. I made a run for the wall and quickly put my two pieces of wood together. I stood up on them, reaching for the top of the wall, and to my horror I was unable to get a grip on the top of the arched brickwork, that's why it had been made that way. Panic struck me; I tried three times – it wasn't going to work. What the fuck was I going to do now? I could see the red-band trustee getting up from the ground; it would take him only a few minutes to walk to the main door when he would need to tell them that I'd made a run for it.

I run to the corner, a couple of hundred yards away, and in desperation make a last attempt to pull myself up over the wall. Being in the corner made it easier, I am over and fall to the ground, up and running, heading for the lakes. They will be out looking for me soon; I must try to find some cover before dark. I head for the cover of trees and bushes. I scramble onto a branch that reaches out over the water's edge just inches from the water, impossible for anyone to walk out and along, checking and looking. I lay there motionless for two hours.

It's dark now; I am safe and can't be seen. I walk around the edge of the lake to the other side. I know where I am now. I know a girlfriend that lives nearby. I head for her house; I am on good terms with the family. I knock on the back door. Her dad opens it.

"Bloody hell, where have you come from? Come on in."

I go in, feeling safe and welcomed. He makes me a cup of tea.

"Where are you headed for?"

"Not really sure at the moment, maybe you can let me have a pair of trousers and a jacket and call a cab for me later."

"Sure I can, that's no problem." He goes off and five minutes later returns with the trousers and jacket, the jacket is a bit too big for me but it will do until I get to the address of the girl that wrote to me saying that I could stay if I wanted to – the girl my mum fixed up for me when on my home leave.

I stay for two more hours and then the daughter returns home; she is a lovely girl and she was pleased to see me, I wish we were still courting, it would have been nice. I liked her very much and she was such a good person, too good for me. I was sad to leave the house; I felt safe there.

The cab came and I was gone, back out into the world of hostility and not belonging. My heart was heavy, not knowing what would become of me now. I tell the cab driver where I want to go; I give him the street name but not the house number. Twenty minutes and we are there. I knock on the door not really knowing what to expect, the door opens and she is there.

"Oh my God!" she says. "What are you doing here?"

"I've come to see you," I said.

"Come in. Where have you come from? I thought you were back in the borstal."

"Yea, I had a little disagreement and decided I didn't want to stay any longer."

"What do you mean?"

"I did a runner – had it over the wall." I said.

"Oh no! What are you going to do now?"

"Stay here with you if that's OK."

"Of course you can, go in and I will make you a drink.

That night was bliss; I had food, drink and sex and I felt safe. What a wonderful feeling, the touch of a woman can make all the difference in the world. 'I love being with a woman,' I thought, 'I never want to be on my own again.' If only that were possible – time to be easy on myself, slow-think a while, be free, be loved, be safe, no problems, no stress, heavenly bliss. If only it could last a lifetime, if only! Not much chance of that in this world.

The days passed and all was easy; no threats or worries yet! I got myself a car and started to go out, moving around, seeing old friends, going to pubs, even got myself some carpentry work, and visited my family once or twice.

"The police have been around," they said, "better not come here too often."

One police officer came on a regular basis, once or twice a week. He got friendly with the family. My younger sister told me that Alfie had found a gun hidden on top of the toilet cistern. Luckily Alfie disposed of it, as a few days later there was a police raid and they had looked up on the toilet cistern. Alfie was convinced that the police had planted it there – who else would have done it?

I started to mix with some really heavy guys now, almost gangsters, similar to the Kray twins, or at least they thought they were: J Kavanagh and Smithy. Kavanagh was a hard man, an ex-boxer; Smithy was a hard-nosed businessman and owned a mini-cab company.

Kavanagh had contacts in the criminal world and the boxing world, and access to guns, as well as contacts in the local police force it turned out. They seemed to have some admiration and respect for me, maybe because I was so unpredictable, young and apparently fearless – if only they knew!

Soon I started working for Smithy as a night driver, and often we would go out to nightclubs for a drink together. I didn't trust him: he was a nasty piece of work and so was Kavanagh. Kavanagh once took me with him to visit a man who apparently had been beating up his wife. We broke into the house in the early hours of the morning and he dragged the man out of bed; he cut him up with a carving knife and told him never to lay a finger on his wife again. Kavanagh was knocking the man's wife off; he hadn't told me that, and he didn't tell me that there were children in the house. After that I decided not to get too involved in his personal affairs again.

I was drinking more and more, and becoming extremely violent at times, with dangerous moments of rage. I also had a gun now, in fact I had two guns, a twelve bore shotgun and a twenty-two calibre bolt-action rifle with a telescope on it and a twelve-shot magazine. One night I took a girl out that I had met, she was only seventeen or eighteen, stunning and beautiful, and so innocent. I met up with Smithy at a nightclub in the West End. Smithy had some mates with him as usual; his mates kept buying me drinks – double brandies. Later in the evening Smithy and the girl disappeared. Smithy had told her that I had gone back to a hotel and I was waiting for them, and she was to go there with him. Smithy took her to the hotel and tried to rape her, but luckily the police were called and she was taken home unharmed.

Smithy's mates had got me drunk and I didn't find out till the next day what had happened. For three nights running I walked along the railway line and waited for Smithy to show up at his mini-cab firm; I could get a good shot at him from the railway bridge. I waited for two hours every night but he never showed up. I started carrying a nine-inch dagger strapped to my left leg in the daytime, always looking out for him. I told people that I was going to kill him and that my intention was to stab him the next time I saw him. It would be eight years before I was to meet up with him again in prison.

Janet, the girl I was living with, told me that her mother took money to the bank every Friday carried in a shopping bag. I arranged for a young lad to snatch the bag from her at the side road on the high street and waited for him in the car. There was eight hundred pounds in the bag and I gave the kid two hundred pounds of it – he was over the moon.

I became very friendly with a guy called George Burgess, a long-distance lorry driver, several years older than me, always smart and well dressed, handsome, and very popular with the ladies. I would go on long trips around the country with him, going to nightclubs, drinking heavily and always chasing the girls. What a life – I loved it! I was very fond of George, he was really good to me and we always got on well. He always carried a gun hidden in the boot of his Jaguar. We both drank too much, and I was the one that always got into fights; he would sometimes use me and often encouraged me to take violent action against people.

One night we were out drinking at a pub, the pub was very crowded and a loud band was playing. The manager refused to serve us. George said, "Tell him we got a gun in the car outside, if he doesn't serve us we will go and get it."

In the process of telling him I grabbed him by the shirt and pulled him across the bar. I got into a big fight and the police were called. George made off in the car because of the gun. I ended up fighting with the police. I was arrested and taken to the local police station, back to court, and back to borstal. My freedom was over.

Chapter 15

Back to borstal. Down the punishment block again, standing in front of the governor, humiliated. What will I say to Dr Ellis? I am very confused, though deep down I know it's the best thing that could happen to me, getting away from the drink, from George, the guns and gang violence, big egos, anger and rage. But I feel devastated and lost. Will I ever be able to lead a normal life, feeling safe and unafraid? I am very tired. I need to rest and think about things. How lucky I am to have my own cell, no noise and no clutter, peace and quiet, away from people. Six days in solitary and I get sent back to the main block.

It isn't long before I receive a letter from Janet. She tells me that she needs to finish with me, sounds like she has a new fella, talks about going water skiing on the lakes just out side the borstal, the ones I took shelter by when I escaped over the wall. I am in the dining room and I can hear the buzzing of the boats going up and down the lake.

Then something snaps inside my head and I am unable to contain myself: I start throwing chairs out through the windows – I've lost it completely.

Everyone scattered in different directions, I just kept throwing chairs – one chair after the other. An officer came running at me. I turned towards him with a chair raised high in the air ready to smash it down on to his head. Fortunately for me he changed his mind and waited until I was finished. I broke seventeen panes of glass before I stopped.

Down the punishment block again I really like it here in solitary confinement. I think I need to stay here permanently, but they won't let me. Alone with myself and my thoughts, I can hear myself think, I can hear my inner voice, the voice of my truth and my spirit – the place where my soul dwells.

I am in great pain, unbearable pain. I go down somewhere deep inside myself searching out my demons, and lose myself in a pit of grief and sorrow. And it's from that place that I find myself going back and remembering the special day many years ago when I was one year old and I was out of my body looking down on my grandmother from above. I begin to cry. I sob like I have never sobbed before. The sobbing overwhelms me and I lose myself to a dark place that calls me. 'Come to me,' it calls, 'and I will give you peace, come to me and I will set you free of this world's suffering.' In desperation I hang onto it for comfort; there is nowhere else for me to go.

I search desperately for a weapon to harm myself. There is nothing, no glass, no steel, no wood, no plastic, nothing, only electricity behind unbreakable plastic that's re-enforced with wire strands, and a small window panel made of the same stuff, high above the cell floor. I take off my shoe and begin to strike at the window panel with blinding rage. Unrelenting, I strike again and again, forcing my will, demanding that it give something up to my desperation. Streams of tears flood from my eyes, they come from an unknown place not accessed before. The floodgates had been opened and nothing would stop the pain and the longing. The inner darkness kept calling me to come; I must go, I must find a way to greet it.

A tiny triangular piece of plastic fell to the floor as if a gift from a dark place, I grabbed at it. There was a strand of wire coming out from the corner edge – this would put to sleep all my sorrows. I quickly stabbed and ripped at my wrist, again and again, deeper and deeper, forcing the skin and flesh to part, desperately searching for the artery that held my blood. The more I ripped into my flesh, the more I sobbed and cried. My eyes filled with tears and through the tears I could see light entering the room, the light getting brighter and brighter. The cell was filled with light, and there in the corner I could see an angel kneeling and weeping. Why was this angel crying? I felt engulfed with a feeling of love. I stopped striking my wrist, I stopped sobbing, and was locked into a moment of eternal love.

The door opened and one of the officers stood there; the light rushed out through the doorway. He staggered and took a step backwards, raising his arm to shield his eyes. He said nothing, sharing the moment with me.

I was taken to the hospital block and treated. Night time never came and the days passed unseen, I had gone off somewhere else for a while, unavailable to the world.

Dr Ellis came to see me down in the cell.

"I am going to put you up in one of the wards for a while, and if you're agreeable I want your permission to use a truth drug on you. Have a think about it," she told me. Truth drug! What the fuck's a truth drug? "I've been reading some of your writing," she said. Most of my writing was unreadable, but I am sure she was capable of reading between the lines.

"Stephan, you are a wonderful and very special person," she tells me, "If everyone in the world was like you the world would be a wonderful place." I couldn't believe what I was hearing, for the first time in my life someone was telling me how wonderful and special I was. She could see me for what I really was, and she was willing to say so. She believed me to be a good person, not a bad person.

"I want to try a truth drug on you," she said, "see if we can break through your resistance and find out what your true feelings are. Will you agree?" I could hardly say no now, after what she had just told me. Maybe that was her way of softening me up in order to get me to agree.

"It's done by the way of an injection in the arm and we will tape record the whole event," she tells me, "It will take about two hours. There will be just you and me and one other medical officer present to help me. You will need to stay in the hospital for a number of weeks before you can go back to the main block. Will you agree?"

"Let me think about it."

I have the whole weekend to relax and recover and think about it. Some days pass and I agree. Dr Ellis sets it up in one of the empty side wards. There are eight beds in the room, four on each side, and four big windows. I notice there are no bars at the windows, and they haven't been cleaned for a while. The beds have no bedding, just mattresses. It doesn't look like it's been used for some time, the air is cold, with a stale smell to it.

No tables and no chairs, one set of double doors, which were unlocked just before we entered. It's bleak, empty, and eerie, just me in one bed and a psychiatrist with a large syringe intending to insert a truth drug into my arm. What will I say? What hidden secrets do I have to tell? I am beginning to get butterflies in my stomach. I wonder how many other people know about this test of truth, there seemed to be a sense of secretiveness about it.

The medical officer won't make eye contact with me. I looked into the doctor's eyes for reassurance; she had a look about her that I had not seen before. I understood that there was an element of risk being taken, but I trusted her and I knew that she was fond of me and would do her best to keep me safe. She was a mature woman, almost totally grey, with eyes that looked into you. I can only describe her as being handsome. There was something that made her different to other women, and I wanted her to love me just like my nan and Mrs B had done many years ago. I wanted to feel safe and cared for by her.

She used the needle in my arm twice. The second time I was off into another world where I found myself strapped onto a white marble table. There were five German Nazi officers in full SS uniform around me. They were sticking needles into me, and trying to get me to talk; I resisted and said nothing. Then my angel appeared and took me off to a safe place.

When I came round there was just the medical officer and myself alone in the room. He said that he would come back in a little while, left and locked the door, leaving me all alone with my thoughts. I wanted to go back and be with my angel; for the first time I had an understanding that my angel was real. I felt concern about what had gone on and what I had said into the tape recorder. I was scared and I didn't want to be alone: I wanted to feel safe, loved; I want to go back to my angel. I knew then that my angel was very much a real part of me – that we were connected by an unbreakable bond.

And I also knew that I didn't want to be in this world. I felt betrayed and abandoned, alone with my evil demons and my sad thoughts of not belonging. I felt scared, as always, unloved and different, with no peace and only a terrible feeling inside – abandonment.

I need to do something, anything! What can I do? I will smash all the windows out with my bare hands!
And that's what I did.

Two medical officers came bursting into the room and grabbed me. They were discussing whether to give me an injection or not, but one of them said that they would need to talk with the doctor first. They moved me down into the basement cells. An officer stayed with me all the time and the cell door was left open.

It was about eight o'clock at night by now and everyone was getting ready to lock up. My hands were ripped and torn, with one of my finger bones showing, and my wrist had started to bleed again, but I wouldn't let them stitch me up before making a deal with them. I demanded that my friend Greg would be allowed to come over and stay with me while they treated me and stitched me up. Greg was allowed to come, and we had a good long chat and a laugh for an hour or so.

That night I had a wonderful peaceful sleep. The next day was like waking up to a new world, a completely different life; I felt I was a different person, a big load had been lifted off my shoulders. I was easy, no stress, no fear, I could see the world and the beauty of being alive.

Dr Ellis will be coming in today on a special visit to see me for a chat, the officer tells me. I can't wait to speak with Dr Ellis and tell her how wonderful I am feeling. Lunchtime comes and I have no desire to eat. Two more hours pass before she arrives. I am still down in the cell; one of the medical officers comes again.

"The doctor is here to see you," he tells me, "She will be down in a few minutes." He leaves the cell door open. She appears.

"How are you Stephan?" she asks.

"I am OK, just a little sore. Sorry about the windows," I tell her.

"Not to worry. They will be fixed on Monday. How are your hands?"

"They're fine, shouldn't take long to heal up."

"Well, as I am sure you are aware it didn't go quite as planned. You made no response whatsoever. I have nothing on the tape to share with you, and I am not surprised you reacted in the way you did."

I told her nothing of the German SS soldiers trying to force information from me, and nothing about the big white angel that came and took me away. Did I need to tell her of these strange happenings?

"So what about you now? I think we can get you out of here, up into one of the small wards. Would you be happy to go up?"

"I don't mind where I go," I replied.

"I can't stay long," she tells me, "I will get one of the officers to take care of you and I will see you on Monday morning and we will talk about what happened yesterday. How does that sound to you?"

"Yea, that sounds fine to me."

"OK, I will leave you in good hands and see you on Monday." She walks away, has a chat with the medical officer and she is gone.

"Let's get you settled in upstairs," he says, "Can you manage on your own?"

"Yea, I am fine," I tell him.

Up we go to one of the wards. Two other guys and four empty beds, one for me and a nice soft mattress, there's a T.V in the ward. I settle in easily, not much to worry about. I lie on the bed watching the TV, as do the other two boys. They don't say anything, just a glance over and a nod of the head. I rest up, thinking 'Why does everything feel so different?' Maybe it's the effect of the drugs. My hands and wrist are lightly bandaged up – half a dozen stitches, nothing to worry about, I will soon heal up. I feel good and fall back into sleep again as if I had not a care in the world.

It's Sunday, I am hungry now and looking forward to lunchtime, how wonderful food is when you're hungry. Life's not so bad and the food is good too. I get talking to one of the other boys called Nick, his leg is in plaster all the way up to his hip and one of his arms is in plaster too. "What happened to you?" I ask.

"Crashed into the back of a lorry on the motorway," he said. It turns out the lorry was parked, no lights, on the hard shoulder and he crashed into it in a stolen car, killing his best friend. Sometimes at night I could hear him crying softly. I didn't really know what to say to him, I felt really sorry for him. I could see that he was torn apart by the death of his friend and it would take many years for him to get over it. He seemed a good lad, intelligent.

My hands heal, the stitches are removed and I am soon back to work with Mr Bennett, just as Dr Ellis said. I realise now that she has really put herself on the line for me, supported me all the way. Reports at the visiting court saved me from a bad end, but I don't think the borstal governor and the establishment were happy about the outcome. It's regarded as a very serious matter when an officer is attacked. Technically he laid his hands on me first in a provoking manner, and I am sure that was argued in my favour. I think she is trying to get me out of here before I get into any more trouble. Other boys here have been sectioned and sent to Broadmoor for far less. Broadmoor is a secure mental hospital for the violent and mentally ill; I think if it wasn't for Dr Ellis I would have gone there long ago.

I was seeing more of Dr Mary Ellis now and we were getting on very well, she was more open with me about what was going on in her life and we were becoming more like friends. She told me that in the second world war German air crew were imprisoned and located in the punishment block where I seem to spend a great deal of my time. German aircrew – maybe my father slept in one of the cells, or maybe he had slept in the same cell as me! I get comfort from the thought.

After a few weeks I was returned to the main block with my wounds healed, feeling brand new – a different person. I seemed to see the world through different eyes now. I watched the other boys causing severe harm to themselves in order to get off work for a few days, my friend Greg being one of them. The boys would put their hands to the edge of the heavy steel-covered doors and have someone slam the door hard on their fingers. 'How stupid they are,' I thought. Greg had found the base of a broken bottle with a jagged, pointed, sharp glass edge to it; he placed his hand over the glass and got one of the other boys to jump on it. The glass cut through two of his tendons – I wish I could have talked him out of it. There are so many crazy desperate boys in this place, full of madness and fear.

I think I have been here long enough now. But have I changed? Have I learnt anything about people and life; and what have I learnt about myself? Is my life going to be easier and different now? I want to be different, and I want to help people with similar problems to mine, I would like to make the world a better place to live. Above all I want to learn, I want to know and learn everything. I want to be creative and positive, I want to embrace life full on and take it in. I want to be open, to belong, free of fear, to be loved, and to be able to love. But first I must learn to read and write – I never did finish reading that book I started when I first came in over two years ago.

I've got my new release date now; I will be going home next week to start a new life, finally getting back home. Things are looking good, a new job to start as a carpenter, a car and money, free to do as I please. Things are going to be different now.

Stephan, aged 20

Looking Back

I truly believe that if I hadn't gone to borstal when I did, getting the help and support I did from Dr Mary Ellis, I would have killed myself. As much as I hated it, I think it was the best thing that could have happened for me at the time. Under the circumstances I have been especially lucky, much luckier than most boys in similar situation. I loved her, and when she died it was a great loss to me. I will always remember her words: 'Stephan you are very special and wonderful person, if everyone in the world was like you the world would be a wonderful place.'

Dr Mary Ellis was greatly responsible for putting a stop to the punishment of bread and water, and the treatment of cold-water baths in borstals.

Acknowledgments

I acknowledge and say a special thank you to the following:

Lucinda and Peter Neall, publishers and facilitators of the Building a Better Future programme
Janet Short (neé Benton-Green) my loyal, dedicated, and best friend
Alex Rose
Ronnie McGrath
Rex Lassalle
Ruskin College, Oxford
The British Legion
Veterans Aid, Stepney, London
Crisis Skylight, London
Richmond Bridge Community Project, London
Alcoholics Anonymous (AA) South West London
Al-Anon Family Group of London
CHT Home Base, London
Central & Cecil Housing trust, London

Without your dedication, courage and support it would not have been possible to complete this book.

And of course myself, always going in search of the light.

I thank you all so much from the deepest place in my heart and soul.

Other books from Leaping Boy Publications:

ABOUT OUR BOYS
A Practical Guide to Bringing the Best out in Boys
Lucinda Neall

This book looks at what motivates and de-motivates boys and how to help them navigate the journey to manhood. Written at the request of parents and youth workers who had read Lucinda Neall's book for teachers, it is packed with practical examples from everyday life.

This unique book avoids the emotionally hobbled, beige type of advice books that flood the market. Lucinda's heart for boys — her advocacy for them — comes across clearly and honestly. If you only buy one non-fiction book this year, get this one.

Simon Langley, Schools Partnership Social Worker

Everyone needs to read this book in order to get a full understanding on how us males tick. It has revolutionized my approach to teaching boys.

Tony Thompson, Boyz 2 Men Project

This book is a fund of common sense: and that is an uncommon commodity.

Peter Villiers, The Police Review

HOW TO TALK TO TEENAGERS
Lucinda Neall

If you have teenagers in your life – at home, at work, or in your neighbourhood – this book may stop you tearing your hair out! It will give you insights into how teenagers tick, and strategies to get their co-operation.

➢ Explains how teenagers see the world
➢ Packed with examples from day-to-to life
➢ Focuses on what to say to get them on board
➢ Includes 'maintaining boundaries' and 'avoiding conflict'
➢ Gives tips on how to stop the nagging and shouting
➢ Encourages adults to see the positive in teenagers
➢ Concise chapter summaries for easy reference

This book says it all. Lucinda has captured the art of dealing with and speaking to teenagers in a fantastic, easy to use guide.

John Keyes, Social Inclusion Manager
Arsenal Football Club

A superb guide – the key issues and techniques of interacting with young people covered in a practical, easy to understand way.

Mark Todd, Chief Executive
Ocean Youth Trust South

Two novels by Susan Day:

THE ROADS THEY TRAVELLED

What did happen to Marcie?

Four girls set out one wartime morning, on a day that will bind them together for years to come. Work and marriage, children and divorce, change and death.

More than seventy years later they are still in touch, and still trying to resolve the tragedy that has been a constant in their lives.

WHO YOUR FRIENDS ARE

It's the 1960s and we meet some of the characters from *The Roads They Travelled*.

Rita – clever, determined, ambitious. Beautiful too.
Pat – none of the above.

Rita is the oldest of five children.
Pat has a more conventional life.

Rita achieves success and money.
Pat has a family.

They say history is written by the winners, but in this case it is by Pat with time on her hands.
What conclusions will she draw?
What judgements will she make?

The TOM AND JAKE Series
Helen MccGwire

Six charmingly written and illustrated little books about Tom and Jake, two little boys who live with their family and animals in an old farm-house in Devon. The stories are based on the experiences of the author's five children during the 1960s, whilst living in the countryside.

Tom and Jake

More About Tom and Jake

Tom and Jake & The Bantams

Tom in the Woods

Tom and Jake & Emily

Tom and Jake & The Storm

Ideal for reading to children, and for revisiting a 1960s childhood.

www.leapingboy.com